Sun bread and Sticky toffee.

DATE DESSERTS FROM EVERYWHERE

SARAH AL-HAMAD

Interlink Books

An imprint of Interlink Publishing Group, Inc.
Northampton, Massachusetts

for Mona, Hessa and Tita

SHORT NOTE ON INGREDIENTS:

Dry, pitted, soft dates used throughout.

Date syrup is available from most whole foods stores and Middle Eastern groceries. You can also make your own: boil equal parts water to dates, add a sprinkling of cinnamon or a little vanilla extract, then pulse in a blender until smooth.

First published 2013 by

INTERLINK BOOKS
An imprint of Interlink Publishing Group, Inc.
46 Crosby Street, Northampton, MA 01060
www.interlinkbooks.com

ISBN: 978-1-56656-921-7 (hardback)
Library of Congress Cataloging-in-Publication data available

Copy editor: Sarah Cobbold
US editor: Leyla Moushabeck
Design: Jacqui Caulton
Production: David Hearn
Location photography: Sarah Al-Hamad
Additional location photography: Matthew Bamberg
Food photography: Kate Whitaker
Food stylist: Rosie Reynolds
Prop stylist: Cynthia Inions
Indexer: Alex Corrin
Illustration on page 15 by Hannah George

Printed and bound in China

Contents

Introduction

A few years ago, I compiled a cultural cookbook of traditional recipes from family and friends in the Gulf. I spent time there, took many photographs, learned to make *machbous* and *balaleet*, some of my favorite local specialties, and talked to people about their love of food. It was a wonderful experience but I never thought I'd write another cookbook.

A few years later, I found myself thinking again of the Gulf and its culinary culture. There was still so much to uncover and so little had been referenced or written about. Here was a culinary culture rich with diverse influences—Persian, Levantine, Ottoman, Indian—and food was so important in regulating daily life, people's relationships, and their kitchens. I could think of many subjects of interest, like our regional saffron- and cardamom-infused *halwa*, or the rustic sesame paste dessert *rahash*, even the benefits of our nomadic dairy culture. But what grabbed me most and excited my taste buds *and* soul, was the story behind our love of dates. Quasi-miraculous, revered, and adored, this ancient, old-world fruit offered so much to so many in the Gulf. Not only because of its "360 uses" but also its healthful and culinary qualities. In my quest to learn more and to bridge and uncover linkages between cultures, I learned of far-away places where dates were enjoyed away from the Middle East; for instance, in my adopted home England, where the luscious sticky toffee pudding is a dessert few can resist. The secret ingredient: dates.

My interest piqued, I embarked on a voyage of date-scovery. I traveled to sunny regions to walk in the footsteps of the Moors in Spain's Elche, to the Liwa Date Festival, and the oasis city of Al Ain in the UAE to marvel at the largest *ithig* (bunch of dates) in the world. I then headed north, to the pretty Cumbrian hamlet of Cartmel in England, famous for its sticky toffee pudding, easily worth the two train rides from London, and finally the westernmost point of my search to the Coachella Valley, California, the newest, date-producing mecca.

That wasn't all. I collected palm frond baskets, mats, and fans from bustling souks, relaxed on palm benches, admired the beautiful white palm artwork, visited an eco-palm leaf house (making a comeback architecturally), and enjoyed my daily morning bowl of porridge with a large spoonful of Basra date syrup.

A home cook, I baked, macerated, poached, boiled, stuffed, fried, mashed, minced, and chopped many, many kilos of soft dates, negotiating the 40 date recipes featured in this book to offer a spectrum of textures and flavors, sweetness levels, and exciting ingredient combinations. In the ensuing culinary alchemy, I witnessed matches I itched to publicize: the well-balanced pairing of dates and nuts; hints of honey and sugar cane in the combining of dates and dairy; the seduction of a pinch of cinnamon, ground cardamom, or ginger in a date dessert; the sublime marriage of dates and chocolate; even the sensible, nutritious union of dates and grains, and many others.

Although date palms have existed for over 6000 years, my trail starts in Mesopotamia around 2000BC. I am thrilled to locate some of the earliest recorded recipes known to us, using both fresh and dried dates. Written on cuneiform tablets in Akkadian, Babylon's early language, these recipes were relatively recently unearthed in Iraq. Experts say these are not everyday recipes; instead they give us an idea of fine dining, Babylonian-style. Dates feature strongly: dates and date juice were used to sweeten food, make vinegar, and adorn spiced cakes and grain porridges, the mainstay of their diet. Dates were so fancy they were added to cakes like *palace cake* (see p. 85) and were offered to honor the gods in temples up and down the Euphrates.

Dates and palms are also mentioned in the writings of the Greek traveler Herodotus from that era, while journeying in Babylon and Egypt. In Ancient Egypt, Herodotus first encounters leavened bread, left to proof in the sun, earning the name "sun bread." My version of sun bread includes honey and dates, two ingredients I know the ancients used in their cooking. I am happy with the result and feel that Herodotus might also approve. The Egyptians refined the use of dates in their cuisine. With spices and dates, they baked celebration breads, and date wine and date beer were popular beverages. Palm wine (from the tree's sap) was used to prepare the body for mummification, while fruit-and-nut cakes were dropped in graves as afterlife snacks. A confection of honey, dates, and spices became the world's first known candy. On wall engravings, palm fronds symbolized fertility and immortality, ennobling the palm as a blessed tree.

In London I toured the exhibition *Afghanistan: Crossroads of the Ancient World* at the British Museum. I was transfixed by delicate objects of beauty at the confluence of ancient cultures, Egyptian, Roman, Indian—the Silk Road—above all a paper-thin, shimmering gold crown, which can be folded and re-assembled (for light traveling monarchs), a genius idea from millennia back. There was also a Roman-Egyptian glass beaker from the 1st century AD, painted in vibrant yellows, blues, reds, and greens. The scene shows women busily harvesting dates, robes hanging off their shoulders, full of movement and energy. I left with a postcard of the beaker for good luck, hopeful that for me too, a harvest lay ahead.

In the 1st century AD, Pliny the Elder's *Natural History* describes at length the date palms of Greece, Persia, Crete, and Sicily. No surprise, seeing as Roman soldiers loved to feast during campaigns, their favorite snack being *satura* cakes of raisins, dates, pine nuts, pomegranate seeds, and honeyed wine.

Around that time, the Greeks named the palm *Phoenix dactylifera*, supposedly after the mythical phoenix bird that rose from the ashes in the deserts of Arabia, and the finger-shaped, sweet fruit of the date palm *daktulos*, meaning "fingers" in Greek—marking it out from other varieties as the "true palm."

Further up the Mediterranean coast, my journey continued in Spain, where I visited Europe's largest date plantation at Elche (*Elx* in Catalan). A short drive inland from Alicante, this plantation flourished in Al-Andalus during the 8–12th centuries, and remains extensive. Palms took well to Spain and the magnificent gardens of the Alhambra in Granada attest to it. The first thing I did was walk the obligatory *Ruta del Palmeral*, a mapped-out two-kilometer stroll around the major orchards (*horts*), to understand the breadth of Elche's Moorish

Palmeral, which in its heyday had over a million palm trees, planted in rows, and fed by clever irrigation channels that remain in use today.

In the dry June heat, the evergreen palms towering above, the light and landscape transported me to the Gulf and I understood why the Moors would have wanted to settle here. I felt very fortunate to be visiting, myself. After the Christian Reconquista of 1236, the Palmeral's fortunes gradually declined and by the 1950s the site was seriously in peril. Fortunately in 2000 the Palmeral was awarded UNESCO World Heritage status. Now protected, it is a pleasure to visit alongside the Museo del Palmeral and the paradisiacal Huerto del Cura, a lush garden of palms, tropical plants, peacocks, and the strangest palm I have ever seen, the seven-branched Imperial Palm, with suckers almost as large as its parent.

Crucially, this helped reintegrate the Palmeral into Elche's heart, which at times seemed to reject this vestige of the past. For lunch I went in search of dates but found only tapas and directions to the nearest supermarket for the famous *delicias de Elche*—almond-stuffed dates wrapped in bacon—world-famous but oddly absent from the town's menus. I wondered why, since the town is surrounded by 200,000 date-bearing palms, and as Spain's native *almendras* (almonds) pair so beautifully with dates. The town also makes a liqueur—*datil*—from dates, cognac, and vanilla. Today it is Elche's spiritual life that is most intimately connected to the date palm: on Palm Sunday the prized blanched palm leaves, grown hooded out of the light, are carried at processions. I couldn't stop noticing and photographing the decorative fronds I saw tied to balconies across Andalucia as I traveled south to Seville.

The same Mediterranean civilization responsible for planting Spain's first palms, the Phoenicians, also carried the date palm to the Canary Islands, the Balearics, Sicily, Malta, and the Levant. In Palermo, Sicily, a large date plantation existed when the Arabs introduced ice-making to the island and something of it still remains. By blending sugar, fruit, and flowers with snow from Mount Etna, the chilled desserts so synonymous with Italy—*granita* and *gelato*—were born. My friend Vittorio from Bari shared a recipe for *gelato ai datteri*, as I found out that a *gelateria* in Ragusa, Sicily, serves date ice cream. I dreamed of a mouth-watering scoop and a trip to Sicily but alas a visit was not on the cards. Further north around Siena there is some evidence that dates were consumed in cakes at religious festivities, perhaps around Christmas time. I went ahead and used them in *biscotti* (see p. 44), with soft figs and crunchy hazelnuts—*la dolce vita.*

In Lebanon, Malta, and North Africa too, there is a long relationship with dates. Malta's rich multicultural past inspired the date-sweet *imqarets* (see p. 51), sold at kiosks at the entrance to the capital Valetta. In Lebanon, Syria, and Palestine, rose-and-orange-fragrant date shortbread, *maamoul* (see p. 67), typifies confections from the region. Similar sweets in Morocco, Algeria, and Tunisia have dates in them, including the fruity Passover spread *haroset* (see p. 36).

Date palms grow from Morocco to India but it is Arabia, with its hot, arid climate, that is most linked with the tree. Growing up in 1970s Kuwait, I would often hear of Basra in Iraq referred to as the Gulf's orchard. Indeed, its plantations were legendary; fed by two rivers (Tigris and Euphrates), they produced excellent dates: *zahidi, khustawi, khadrawi,* and *barhi,* among the fine specimens. My family owned date farms—and a home—there, as did many Kuwaitis in the early 1900s. My paternal great-grandfather, a merchant, traded in dates and other crops. My aunt, who spent a fair deal of time there, loved the place. A piece of home close to Kuwait's northern border and culturally familiar, Basra was once a welcoming oasis. In 1913, Paul Popenoe wrote that Basra had eight million palms, the largest date-growing region in the world! With the ensuing decades of strife all would change and neighborly ties would be severed. The devastation to Iraq's ecosystem, marshes, and date plantations, casualties of war, and neglect would all sadly ensue. Having little control over its fate, my family's plantation fell into disuse.

Today, Asia's largest date center is the Al-Hasa oasis in Saudi Arabia, with three million cultivated date

Kora Creek, Basra.

palms, making the country one of the world's major date producers, after Egypt and Iran. So plentiful are dates in Arabia that this "bread of the desert" is enjoyed in many ways: a purist would insist that a date be enjoyed fresh, left in the mouth to release its flavors, then washed down with water or Arabic *gahwa*, a concentrated, strong coffee; others copiously enjoy them in cooked Arabian desserts

Date Palms, Basra.

like *tamriya* (see p. 114) or *rangeenak* (see p. 128), spartan in their simplicity, with no added sugar—at most, a pinch of ground cardamom (*hail*).

Medicinally, the fruit's healing properties are well known—of note, its benefits to seafarers. In the days of pearl diving and long sea voyages, dates were an essential part of a sailor's diet and helped prevent scurvy (which afflicted European sailors). Dates were also believed to cure coughs, alleviate lower-back pain, and help nursing mothers produce abundant milk. Nowadays, a breakfast of date syrup and tahini soaked up with warm flatbread provides fuel for the day, and the rice and fish dish *muhammar simach*, tinged purple and caramel-sweet from date syrup, is still a popular Friday-lunch dish in the Gulf.

The same devotion to dates is evident in the UAE, my next stop, increasingly a regional leader and date-growing center. I was excited to be there. In terms of date production, the city of Al Ain is the hub: I visited the town, its oasis a green cocoon of lush orchards fed by ancient water channels (*falajs*), and toured an impressive date-sorting factory, leaving with an armful of date goodies to take home. But my main reason for visiting was the Liwa Date Festival, an annual celebration of all things date-related. It is a long drive south from Abu Dhabi but I knew I had reached the Empty Quarter desert when the pale desert morphed into striking, shape-shifting pink sand dunes. This was where and why the explorer Wilfred Thesiger fell in love with the desert.

It was July and very hot outside but also the time of the harvest. The festival's large tents enclose a world of dates. Local farmers, many of them women, compete to win cash prizes for best-tasting dates and largest bunch (*ithig*). I was offered a drink of fresh *bisr* juice, pressed when the dates are at their yellow crunchiest. This amber nectar is wonderfully refreshing. Everywhere on tables, palm baskets overflowed with fresh dates, tagged with the farmer's name. There were women energetically weaving palm baskets, fans, and mats; palm offshoots to buy; and palm-leaf houses to explore; ingeniously mobile and sustainable, they reminded me of the portable gold crown I'd seen at the British Museum a few months earlier. Not long after my trip to Liwa, the *Arish: Palm Leaf Architecture* exhibition at the Royal Geographical Society reunited me with the scenic Liwa oasis during the wettest April on record. I smiled at the irony of an elegant Arish house reconstructed in these verdant London gardens.

North Africa's love affair with dates is equally ancient and, in the 16th and 17th centuries, helped introduce dates to northern Europe through trade and commerce. Queen Elizabeth I and Sultan Ahmad al-Mansur of Morocco were allies (against the Spanish and Ottomans) and traded in sugars, almonds, and dates—for English cloth and sometimes a lute for the sultan. In 1551, the first English merchant ship reached Morocco and many more followed in either direction. Dates and dried fruits entered the medieval kitchen and homes of Europe's wealthy. Elizabethan cookbooks list dozens of custards and pies made with cooked dates, like *custard lombard*, a pie of cream, eggs, and dates (a cousin of the quiche) or the tasty *spinnach and date fritters*, among others; expensive imports like dates were status symbols. Luckily, in modern Britain dates continue to be central to one particular dish, eaten up and down the country but in particular after a long day's hiking in the hills of Cumbria. There are few things more comforting to the spirit than a warm *sticky toffee pudding* (see p. 77), my daily treat on my visit to the area. Without those early trade links with Europe, this dessert would not have come to be so wonderfully sticky.

North Africa continued to be a major date center, exporting dates to northern Europe, its two most significant varieties being the large, succulent, and chewy *medjool* and Tunisia's semi-dry "date of light," the *deglet noor*—eventually California's top two dates. Originally reserved for Moroccan royalty, the medjool date was almost wiped out by disease in the early 1900s (in the 1760s palms brought over to South America by the Spaniards, most probably seeds from

plantations at Elche or Andalucia, failed to prosper). With the blessing of the local Moroccan sheikhs, a few healthy offshoots were sent off to be planted in California, where they grew healthy and thrived, producing the great date boom of the 1920s. Their heirs now populate the Coachella (California) and Bard (Arizona) valleys. Today, the National Date Festival (the largest date event in the world) held every year in Indio, celebrates California's connection to the tree in a totally American way, with pageants and beauty contests. Morocco's counterpart three-day celebration takes place in Erfoud, in the south of the country.

I love this tale of transfer and transplantation: native trees sent far away to an alternative universe of shiny strip malls and milkshakes, date farms and *palmeros* (palm workers) to re-invent itself. In California, the *medjool* is the Cadillac of dates and because of its size, flavor, and texture is the world's best-known date. Hearing California date farmers use Arabic terms to describe the life cycle of the date is another cultural oddity: *kimri* dates are immature, green, and unripe, ideally hooded against the strong sun and preying birds; *khalal* are fully-formed and crunchy, reddish or yellow—some varieties are eaten at this stage although they will taste astringent; *rutab* are half-ripe and semi-soft, part-yellow, part-amber—they are fragile to pick but edible and often available at Middle Eastern grocers; finally, most dates are harvested when sticky-sweet, wrinkled, and dark brown with the longest shelf life, at the *tamr* stage. At this point, the date is 70 percent sugar, in easily digestible form, rich in vitamins A and B and minerals like iron, calcium, and magnesium.

I am moved by how human the date palm is. Palms are either male or female, only the latter bearing fruit. Once upon a time the tree was wind-pollinated but the process was slow and haphazard, so man took things in hand, collecting pollen from the male to sprinkle onto the female flowers every spring. Thus the tree was domesticated and the male put to work. A single male tree can pollinate up to 50 females and some farmers only keep them for that purpose. As the trees mature, young offshoots start to grow at the base. Once carefully separated and replanted, they too can become mothers or fathers. At five to seven years old, a pollinated palm will start to bear fruit, up to 220lb/100kg a year, for about 75 years or even a century—a healthy human lifespan! Palms hate the rain, which can ruin the pollen, but love having their feet submerged in fresh water and their heads in the sun and heat. A sociable bunch, they thrive in company, suffer if neglected, and are prone to sickness and overheating. Their trunks are made of faux wood, a mesh of plant fibers, making palms technically a grass, lightweight and flexible enough to withstand very strong winds. The tree's heart—the terminal leaf bud at the top—is the nerve center (a little like the human brain) and survival depends on its preservation.

The week before I wrapped up the project, my sister called with the poignant news that my grandfather's plantation in Iraq was to be sold. After years of trying to regain control of the land, my cousins received an offer to sell and it fell to us to make the final decision. The majority voted to sell; I didn't want to be difficult so also agreed. It was bittersweet to let the land go—for sentimental reasons, I still feel attached to it. I can imagine my aunt and father, my grandparents too, walking the lush, fertile patchwork of palms, sitting in their shade, sipping sweet, red tea in the afternoon glow. I know this is impractical nostalgia, but I feel connected to this place I have never seen. With the city fast encroaching, it would have been impossible to maintain the plantation as

KING SOLOMON TREE

This most famous male palm was imported from Arabia in 1912 and established the almost unbelievable record of caring for over 400 female date-bearing palms, resulting in 3,600,000 offspring each year.

© 1960 Ferris H. Scott, Santa Ana, CA.

an agricultural plot. It's time the land gave way to new life, different faces, and other functions but my childhood connection to the mythical garden of palms is still real to me. Unconsciously, it must have fueled and driven this project. Like my date trail, I too am a link in the chain.

This patchwork of sweet recipes and history, a relaxing forest of evergreen paths, from desert to city and countryside, east to west and north to south, has sustained, fascinated, and nourished me as it has countless travelers on arduous journeys. On this voyage, in the footsteps of date palms everywhere, I have learned that nothing is as local as we believe, that people are always connected by ideas, trade, knowledge, and discoveries. The Moors left Spain a richer place and a lasting legacy of date palms beautifully frames Andalucia; it also connected them more deeply to their faith. The Californians revived an almost extinct palm, restoring it to life in their own unique way, while building a modern industry from it. As ever, the Europeans have greatly prospered from trade with the East, reaping the benefits of strong naval and strategic ties—and in the process, improving their diets immeasurably. Date palms have been cultivated for centuries and continue to prosper and yield ever stronger and healthier harvests, aided by 21st-century technologies like in vitro cultivation and pest control, the old helped by the new, comfort for humankind, who can continue to enjoy this sustaining, luscious, and nutritious fruit, now more available than ever, for many more centuries.

More on dates ...

Arish: Palm-Leaf Architecture by Sandra Piesik (Thames & Hudson).

Dates: A Global History by Nawal Nasrallah (Reaktion Books).

Date Growing in the Old World and the New World by Paul Bowman Popenoe (General Books).

Eric Hansen in *Saudi Aramco World*, 2004.

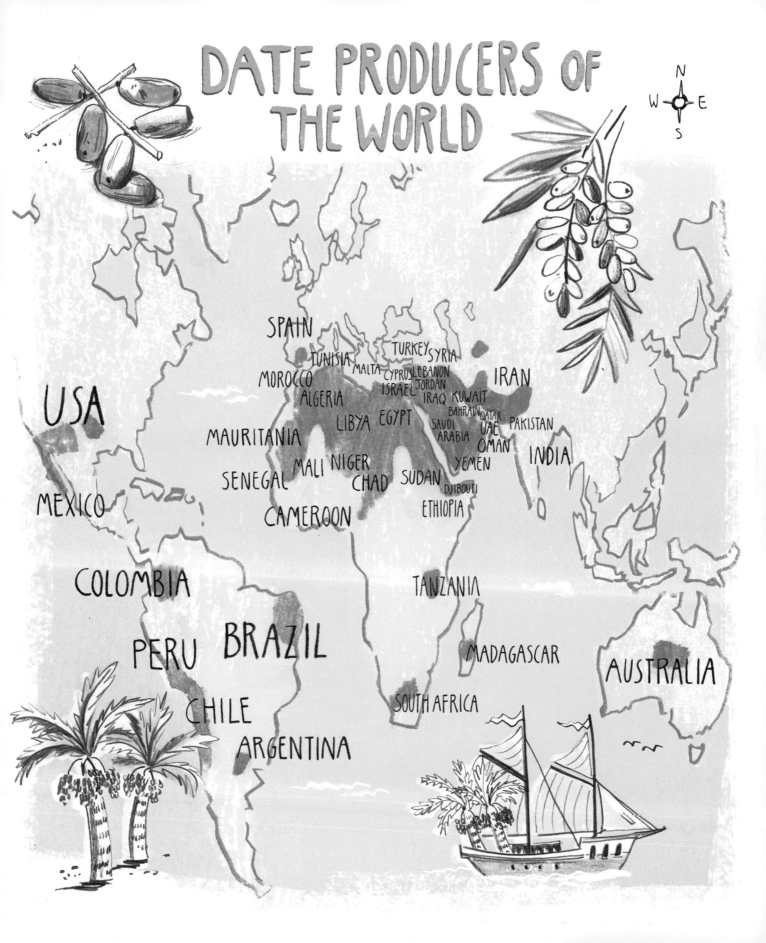

Breads and spreads

Grains were one of the most important food sources to the ancient Egyptians, particularly in the form of bread. They ate over thirty different types of bread and were the first to use leavening agents—Herodotus records eating sourdough in Luxor around 450BC. Like the Mesopotamians, they used wheat, barley, or corn as a base and added dates, spices, honey, and seeds for important occasions. The breads were shaped into rounds, crescents, or crosses and were often scored on top. *Shamsi* bread, meaning "sunny" in Arabic, received its name after the ancients left their loaves to rise in the sun. It remains the staple loaf, baked in clay ovens throughout Upper Egypt today.

This dense, fragrant, sweet bread, inspired by the ancient recipe, keeps for days and is perfect for breakfast, slathered with cream cheese, or at any time with a cup of tea.

Sun Bread

DATE, SPICE, AND HONEY LOAF

SERVES 8

9 tbsp/4½oz/120g butter, softened, plus extra for greasing

¼ cup/2oz/50g light brown sugar

2 tbsp honey

6 large eggs, separated

⅔ cup/8oz/225g all-purpose/plain flour

1 tbsp ground nutmeg

1 tbsp ground cinnamon

11oz/300g dates, roughly chopped

5oz/150g almonds, roughly chopped

Preheat the oven to 350F/180C/gas 4. Lightly butter and line the base of a 2lb/900g loaf pan.

Beat the sugar, honey, and egg yolks together for a few minutes until thick and pale yellow. Add the butter and beat again until blended. In a separate large bowl, whisk the egg whites until they form soft peaks. Using a large metal spoon, carefully fold the egg whites into the yolk mixture.

Sift the flour and spices into the bowl, then fold in the dates and almonds until well incorporated.

Pour the batter into the loaf pan and bake for 1 hour or until a skewer inserted into the center of the bread comes out clean.

Remove from the oven and leave to cool in the pan. Serve warm or at room temperature.

This is a nourishing loaf, textured with healthy seeds and loaded with fiber, with the dates adding just the right amount of sweetness. Making bread is highly satisfying and you'll be surprised just how easy, too. For this very versatile recipe, I've used sunflower and caraway seeds, but you could try adding pumpkin or poppy seeds and substituting some of the wholewheat/wholemeal flour for rye. Perfect with soup, a salad, or strong cheese and chutney.

SUNFLOWER SEED, CARAWAY, AND DATE BREAD

MAKES 1 LOAF

½ tbsp active dry yeast

2 tbsp date syrup

1 tbsp sunflower oil, plus extra for greasing

1⅔ cup/9oz/250g wholewheat/wholemeal flour

1 cup/5½oz/150g white flour, plus extra for kneading

2 tsp salt

2 tsp caraway seeds

2oz/50g sunflower seeds

7oz/200g dates, roughly chopped

Dissolve the yeast in a scant ¼ cup/50ml of warm water, then stir in one tablespoon of the date syrup. Set aside in a warm place for 10 minutes, until the mixture starts to froth. Meanwhile, mix the remaining syrup with the sunflower oil.

Tip the flours, salt, and seeds into a large bowl. Make a well in the center, then pour in the yeast and oil mixtures. Mix well with your fingers, gradually adding another ¾–1 cup/200–250ml water while you work the mass into a dough. If the dough is still floury, add another tablespoon or two of water.

Transfer to a lightly floured work surface and knead for 10–15 minutes until smooth and elastic. Place the dough in a lightly greased bowl, cover, and leave to rise for one hour or until doubled in size.

Preheat the oven to 425F/220C/gas 7 and lightly oil a 2lb/900g loaf pan.

When the dough has risen, knock it back with your fists, then fold in the dates. Place the dough into the oiled loaf pan, cover, and leave to rest for a further 20 minutes.

Once the dough has proofed, bake for 30–45 minutes until risen and golden. To check whether it's done, tap the base of the loaf—if it sounds hollow, that's a sign that the bread has cooked through. If the top starts to brown before then, cover loosely with a sheet of foil.

Remove the loaf from the pan and leave to cool fully on a wire rack.

The Gulf

In the Gulf, date shops get very busy in the run-up to the month of fasting, Ramadan. People start to prepare weeks before, stocking up on crates of fresh dates for their households but also to give away. Sold by the kilogram, dates are stored in freezers then thawed the day before eating. At sunset, when the iftar canon is heard over the radio or tv, families and friends sit down to break fast with a soft, sweet date or two to restore sugar levels. Outside, the deserted streets have never been so quiet...

غرة
١,٥٠

These scones are really fluffy, delicious and, as with all scones, best eaten straight out of the oven. The addition of dates lends just the right amount of sweetness, although those with a sweeter palate may want to add a tablespoon or two of sugar. The buttermilk activates the raising agent and imparts a lovely grainy texture to the scones but you could always substitute milk if you wished. In the unlikely event you have some leftovers, freeze the scones as they don't keep well. Then you can simply reheat when needed.

Light-as-a-feather Scones

BUTTERMILK AND DATE SCONES

MAKES 6 SCONES

2 cups/9oz/250g all-purpose/ plain flour, plus extra to dust

2½ tsp baking powder

2 tbsp superfine/caster sugar (optional)

4 tbsp/2oz/60g butter, chilled and diced

½ cup/4fl oz/125ml buttermilk, at room temperature

4oz/100g dates, finely chopped

1 egg yolk, lightly beaten, for glazing

Preheat the oven to 425F/220C/gas 7 and line a baking tray with wax/greaseproof paper. Sift the flour, baking powder, sugar (if using), and a pinch of salt into a large bowl. Tip in the diced butter.

Rub the butter into the flour with your fingertips for about 5 minutes, until the mixture is pale golden and resembles breadcrumbs. Pour in the buttermilk and mix very gently using your fingers or a fork to form a soft dough.

Tip the dough onto a lightly floured surface, fold in the dates, then pat the dough down and fold once or twice to form a 1in/3cm thick round. Leave the dough to rest for half an hour.

Cut the dough into six rounds using a 2in/5cm cookie cutter or the rim of a jam jar. Place on the baking tray and brush the tops lightly with the beaten egg yolk.

Bake for 10–12 minutes until firm to the touch and golden brown on top.

Enjoy warm with clotted or whipped cream and your favorite jam—Muna's Magical Jam (p. 41) is particularly good!

Most of the bakers in the Gulf come from Central Asia, particularly Afghanistan, and follow the Persian methods of baking bread. Visiting in the July morning heat made the camera lens fog up, but despite the heat, the bakers worked incredibly fast, swinging dough overhead then slapping it into the *tandoor*, the wood-fired oven. They baked hundreds of loaves, keeping pace while a line of customers formed outside, a bread cozy or loose newspaper pages in hand—the bakery sells bread and nothing else. By 9AM the baking was over and the next day's dough was underway...

This flatbread with its subtle toffee flavor is commonly eaten at breakfast with sharp white cheese.

Khubz bil tamr

DATE-FLAVORED FLATBREADS

MAKES 6 FLATBREADS

1 tsp active dry yeast

3 tbsp date syrup

2 cups/9oz/250g all-purpose/plain flour

1 tsp salt

1 tbsp vegetable oil

sesame seeds, to sprinkle

Dissolve the yeast in a scant ¼ cup/50ml of warm water and stir in one tablespoon of the date syrup. Set aside in a warm place for 10 minutes or until the mixture starts to froth.

Mix the flour and salt together in a large bowl. Make a well in the center, then pour in the yeast mixture and remaining date syrup and mix well. Pour in the vegetable oil and about ½ cup/100–150ml of water, gradually—you might not need all of it, so add a little at a time.

Transfer the dough to a lightly floured work surface and knead for 10–15 minutes until soft and smooth. Place the dough in a lightly oiled bowl, cover and leave to rise until doubled in size.

Knock the dough back, then divide it into six or eight equal portions (depending on the size you're after). You can also use a scale to weigh out perfectly equal sized loaves. Roll each portion into a ball—if they're sticky, sprinkle a little more flour on the work surface. Transfer the balls to a baking sheet, cover, and leave to rest for a further 20 minutes. With a brush, moisten each bun-top with a little water, then sprinkle with sesame seeds (the water will make the seeds stick).

Heat a large frying pan. Using your palms, stretch and flatten each ball out as thinly as you can, to pita size. Dry fry the loaves one at a time, turning over a few times until risen, crispy, and golden.

Stack the flatbreads on a serving plate, then cover with a dish towel to keep them warm until ready to eat. They are at their best eaten warm and fresh out of the pan.

Haroset (or *charoseth*) is a fruit and nut paste eaten at Passover, its color and texture reminiscent of the mortar used by slaves in ancient Egypt. Ashkenazi *haroset* is traditionally basic, using apples and walnuts. The Sephardi version, although dependent on local ingredients, is likely to be more sumptuous with chestnuts, almonds, figs, dates, and raisins; it is sometimes known as Venetian *haroset* and sweet red Passover wine is often added. I learned about *haroset* while researching the culinary culture of Jews in North Africa, and later via two Cairo-born friends, Sonia and Danielle, who generously shared their recipe with me. At Passover, this spread is enjoyed very simply on unleavened crackers, but it's also delicious on crispy sourdough bread with cheese and herbs. I used a food processor but traditionalists may prefer everything hand-chopped, to add symbolic texture.

Bejeweled Haroset

DATE, WALNUT, AND APRICOT SPREAD

SERVES 4–6

5½oz/150g dates

2½oz/75g dried cherries

2½oz/75g dried apricots

½ tsp cinnamon

1 apple, peeled, cored, and grated

2 tbsp date syrup or honey

2 tbsp walnuts or pine nuts, toasted and chopped

In a saucepan, heat all the ingredients except the nuts with ¼ cup/60ml water, until softened and mushy. Transfer to a food processor and blend to a paste. Sprinkle over the walnuts or pine nuts, if using.

Refrigerate until ready to eat, then serve in a bowl with crackers or bread.

Let the bird of loudest lay
On the sole Arabian tree,
Herald sad and trumpet be;
To whose sound chaste wings obey

William Shakespeare, **Love's Martyr**, The Phoenix and Turtle, 1601

As a blend of Gujarati and Persian cuisines, Parsi cuisine is known for its bold flavors, mild spiciness and use of dried fruit. It centers around family-based cooking and reminds me of the Gulf dishes I ate growing up. These sweet flatbreads are traditionally eaten during Norouz, the ancient festival of the spring equinox, when night and day are equally long. The festival also marks the Persian New Year and the start of spring.

Kajoor ni-ghari

COCONUT AND DATE-STUFFED NAANS

MAKES 4–6 NAANS

1 tsp active dry yeast

3 tbsp date syrup

2 cups/9oz/250g all-purpose/plain flour, plus extra for kneading

1 tsp salt

1 tbsp vegetable oil

4 tbsp dried shredded/desiccated coconut

4oz/100g dates, very finely chopped

vegetable oil, for frying

Dissolve the yeast in a scant ¼ cup/50ml of warm water, then stir in 1 tablespoon of the date syrup. Set aside in a warm place for 10 minutes until the mixture starts to froth.

Mix the flour and salt together in a large bowl. Make a well in the center, add the yeast mixture and remaining date syrup, and mix well. Pour in the oil and about ½ cup/100–150ml of water gradually—you might not need all of it, so add a little at a time.

Transfer the dough to a lightly floured work surface and knead for 10–15 minutes until soft and smooth. Place the dough in a lightly oiled bowl, cover, and leave to rest until doubled in size.

Knock the dough back, then divide it into four or six equal portions (depending on the size you're after). You can use a scale to weigh out perfectly equal sized portions. Roll each portion into a ball and transfer to a baking sheet to rest for a further 20 minutes.

Meanwhile, mix the coconut, dates, and 1 tablespoon of water in a bowl. With your palms, roll the mixture into four or six small date-coconut balls, depending on how many dough balls you have.

With a lightly floured rolling pin, roll each dough ball out as thinly as you can, place a coconut-date ball in the center, then gather up the edges, pinch, and twist to seal the filling.

Heat a large pan with a tablespoon or two of vegetable oil. Using your palms, flatten each naan, then stretch it out thinly. Fry one at a time, turning over a few times, until crispy and golden.

Remove from the pan and drain any excess oil on paper towels. Enjoy warm.

Our neighbour and friend Muna makes delicious date marmalade with fresh dates and oranges from her fragrant garden in Kuwait. Her homemade jam is the inspiration for this one. Dates contain little pectin so a fruit stock, made from apples, pears, or oranges, is essential to help the jam set. Otherwise a hard slab of toffee is likely—I learned this the hard way. Chunky or smooth, this versatile jam can be enjoyed on a generously buttered slice of crisp brown bread or alongside cheese and cold cuts. Jars of jam also make perfect seasonal gifts. In the Levant region, a popular date and rose petal jam will typically have a lone blanched almond hidden in the middle of the jam.

Muna's Magical Jam

DATE, PEAR, AND STEM GINGER JAM

MAKES 4 MEDIUM JARS

11oz/300g dates, chopped

juice ½ lemon

2lb 4oz/1kg pears, peeled, cored, and chopped

2½ cups/500g granulated sugar

¼ tsp ground ginger

3 pieces preserved stem ginger, finely chopped

Begin by sterilizing the jars. Wash them in warm soapy water, then dry in the oven at 300F/150C/gas 2 for 10 minutes. Alternatively, run them through a hot dishwasher cycle before letting them dry completely. Meanwhile, whizz the dates and lemon juice together in a food processor until very finely chopped, then set aside.

Place the pears in a heavy-bottomed pan and cover with 2¼ cups/500ml water. Cook gently over low heat for about 10 minutes until the pears soften. Add the sugar and stir continuously until dissolved, then increase the heat and bring to a boil without stirring.

Boil for 15 minutes or so until the jam thickens and reaches setting point (the pears will turn very pale and the mixture will thicken and bubble up). To test, drop a little jam onto a chilled plate; it should wrinkle when pressed with a finger. If not, keep cooking and test again at one-minute intervals.

Once set, stir in the date purée, ground ginger, and chopped stem ginger. Cook on low heat for one minute, then leave to cool slightly in the pan before carefully pouring into the jars. Cover immediately with lids and store in a dry cupboard away from direct sunlight. Refrigerate once opened.

Cookies, brownies,
and slices

Biscotti are twice-baked biscuits, great for dunking into coffee or enjoying on their own. They should be crispy and a little hard to bite into, but not teeth-breaking. Pistachios are not easy to source, and are expensive, so as an alternative, try using hazelnuts instead. They are just as yummy and perhaps even more authentic, Italy being one of the world's largest hazelnut producers. The word "date" first appeared in Europe around the time of Marco Polo's travels along the Silk Road in 1290 and the West's first encounter with many of the fragrant spices and dried fruits we cook with today. A ray of Italian joy.

Crunchy Tuscan Biscotti

PISTACHIO, DATE, AND FIG BISCOTTI

MAKES 24 COOKIES

2 cups/9oz/250g all-purpose/plain flour

½ cup/4oz/100g fine raw/golden caster sugar

1 tsp baking powder

zest 1 lemon

3 large eggs, lightly beaten

4oz/100g dried figs, chopped

4oz/100g dates, chopped

4oz/100g pistachios or hazelnuts, whole

Preheat the oven to 340F/175C/gas 4 and line a large baking tray with wax/greaseproof paper.

Mix the flour, sugar, baking powder, and lemon zest together in a large bowl. Make a well in the center and gradually pour in the beaten eggs, mixing until the dough takes shape. The dough should feel sticky but firm. Fold in the fruit and nuts, making sure they are well distributed.

Divide the dough into four parts. Wet your hands to keep them from sticking, then roll the dough back and forth a few times into sausage-shaped logs about 2in/5cm thick. Place on the baking tray, press gently with your palms to flatten slightly, then bake for 30–35 minutes until firm and pale golden.

Remove from the oven; when cool enough to handle, use a bread knife to cut the biscotti, lengthways, into slices about ½in/1cm thick.

Lay the biscotti back on the tray and bake for 8–10 minutes. Turn over and bake for another 8–10 minutes or until crisp and golden on both sides.

Leave to cool on a wire rack before storing in an airtight container.

In Arabic, *ful-sudani* means peanuts. Aunt Saniya grew up in Sudan, where snacking on handfuls of peanuts and dates is the regional equivalent of gorging on jelly beans. She told me about Sudan's palm region, the local date varieties there, and *madidat al-balah*, a rich Sudanese dessert eaten to mark life events like births and weddings. These deliciously nutty macaroons accent sweet and salty flavors and prove that the crunchy-salty-sweet combo of peanuts and dates really works. It's an easy recipe and I absolutely adore it.

Ful Sudani Macaroons

PEANUT-DATE COOKIES

MAKES 25–30 MACAROONS

2 large egg whites

¼ cup/2oz/50g light brown sugar

½ tsp vanilla extract

7oz/200g peanuts, roasted and salted

4oz/100g dates, finely chopped

Preheat the oven to 350F/180C/gas 4 and line two baking trays with wax/greaseproof paper.

Pour the egg whites into a large bowl. Using an electric hand mixer or whisk, beat the egg whites until stiff peaks form. Add the sugar and vanilla and whisk again until fully combined and the mixture is a light brown color.

Pulse the peanuts in a food processor a few times, then tip the crumbled peanuts into the egg white mixture with the chopped dates. Carefully fold in the peanuts and dates using a large metal spoon. The mixture will have the consistency of a paste.

Using a teaspoon or pastry/piping bag with a ½in/1cm tip, measure out equal sized cookies on the tray, leaving a generous gap between each, as they will spread when baked.

Bake for 15 minutes until nicely golden with the edges slightly darker. The center will feel springy but firms up to a lovely chewy consistency once cool. Cool slightly on the tray, lift them off with a spatula, and transfer to a wire rack to cool completely.

Everybody loves a flapjack. These chewy oat bars are packed full of sweet dates, tangy mango, and nutty pumpkin seeds and it's hard not to love the gleaming colors: pale yellow, dark green, and rich brown. They're easy and quick to make, are a great energy snack, and lots of fun to bake with kids. In the 1950s the phrase "soppy date" was used affectionately to tease someone who was being silly or overly sentimental, and mothers were known to use it with their kids.

Dazzling Oat Bars

MANGO, DATE, AND PUMPKIN SEED FLAPJACKS

MAKES 15 SQUARES

¼ cup/2oz/50g light brown sugar

5 tbsp/2½oz/75g butter

2 tbsp golden syrup

2 tbsp date syrup

1 cup/6oz/175g rolled/porridge oats

2oz/50g soft dried mango, roughly chopped

4oz/100g dates, roughly chopped

2 tbsp pumpkin seeds

Preheat the oven to 340F/175C/gas 4. Grease and line a shallow 8in/20cm baking pan.

Put the sugar, butter, and syrups into a deep, heavy-based saucepan and bring to a boil, stirring continuously to stop the sugar from catching. Remove from the heat and whisk until emulsified and a glossy brown.

Tip in the oats, chopped fruit, and seeds and mix well until everything is well-coated in the buttery syrup. Tip the mixture into the tray and, using your fingers (it's easier than using a spoon), push the mixture out evenly into all four corners. Bake for 20 minutes or until the edges are golden brown and the center is slightly soft.

Remove from the oven and leave to cool completely before turning out and cutting into squares.

South of Sicily and east of Tunisia, Malta's name comes from *meli*, the Greek word for honey. This tiny, honey-sweet island has been a meeting place for many cultures over the centuries; the Phoenicians, Greeks, Romans, Arabs, Berbers, Normans, Sicilians, and British have all sojourned here. In 909AD, Malta came under Fatimid rule as part of the emirate of Sicily. Like Elche's Palmeral, the island's date palms remain a symbol of its multicultural past. Famous for its unique honey, Malta is also home to the date *imqaret*. This much-loved street food, a close cousin of the Moroccan *maqrout*, is sold from street stalls at the entrance to Valetta, the Maltese capital.

Imqarets

MALTESE DATE DIAMONDS

MAKES 20 FRITTERS

scant 1½ cups/7oz/200g all-purpose/plain flour

1 tsp pumpkin pie/mixed spice

1 tbsp superfine/caster sugar

8 tbsp/4oz/100g butter, chilled and cubed

1 tbsp orange blossom water

vegetable oil for frying

1 tbsp milk, for brushing

For the date paste

7oz/200g dates, roughly chopped

1 tbsp orange blossom water

1 tsp cinnamon

1 tbsp sunflower oil

zest 1 lemon

Mix the flour, spice, and sugar together in a large bowl. Add the butter and rub it in using your fingertips until the mixture resembles breadcrumbs. Add the orange blossom water and 1 tablespoon of water, then knead until the mixture comes together to form a soft dough. If the dough isn't pliable enough, add another tablespoon of water, but don't over-knead the pastry. Cover and rest in the fridge for 20 minutes or so.

Meanwhile, prepare the date paste. Place all of the ingredients in a small pan and soften the dates over a low heat, squashing the dates with the back of a spoon until mushy. Tip the paste into a bowl and chill in the fridge.

When the dough is ready, bring it back to room temperature, then lightly roll it out into two large, thin rectangular sheets. Trim off any uneven edges with a sharp knife. Roll out the cooled date paste into two or three long, thin sausage shapes, a little shorter than the pastry sheets.

To assemble the *imqaret*, take one of the pastry sheets and lay the date paste down in rows, starting about ¾in/2cm away from the edge and leaving a generous gap between each. Brush a little milk around and between the rows of date paste, then carefully lift the other pastry sheet and place it on top to cover the filling. The filling will protrude. Using a sharp knife, cut the pastry along each row, then diagonally into triangles. pinching the edges together to seal the filling.

In a deep, wide pan, heat enough oil to shallow fry the fritters in batches for a few minutes on each side until golden. Drain off any excess oil on paper towels, then transfer to a warm oven until ready to serve. Alternatively, bake in the oven at 340F/175C/gas 4 for 10–15 minutes until pale golden.

My friends Zar and Barbara live in Naperville, a suburb of Chicago. A few years ago I visited them during a particularly harsh winter, and I was entirely unprepared for just how cold it would be. As it turned out, we spent our days cozily indoors, chatting and baking these yummy spice cookies, which Barbara makes a big batch of every winter, ahead of the holidays. Our baking sessions remain indelibly etched in my memory, a sweet and spicy cloud of warmth and enduring friendship. When one of my friends baked these recently, the filling was so popular with her kids, she wasn't sure they'd end up with cookies. If you can keep hands (and mouths) away from the filing, the cookies will reward you amply.

Barbara's Festive Gems

DATE AND FIG ROLLS FOR THE HOLIDAYS

MAKES 30 COOKIES

9 tbsp/4½oz/120g butter

½ cup/4oz/100g superfine/caster sugar

2 cups/9oz/250g all-purpose/plain flour

1½ tsp baking powder

1 tsp vanilla extract

zest ½ lemon

2 large eggs

3 tbsp milk

1 tbsp confectioner's/icing sugar

1 tsp sesame seeds, to sprinkle

For the fruit filling

1 pear, peeled, cored, and chopped

5½oz/150g dates

2½oz/75g dried figs

1oz/25g glacé or dried cherries

½ tsp allspice

½ tsp cinnamon

grating nutmeg

1 tbsp date syrup or honey

juice ½ lemon

Beat the butter and sugar together until light and creamy. Stir in the flour, baking powder, vanilla, and lemon zest and finally the eggs, one at a time, to bring everything together. Wrap the dough in plastic wrap/cling-film and leave to rest in the fridge for at least two hours.

To make the filling, whizz all the ingredients in a food processor until finely chopped.

Preheat the oven to 350F/180C/gas 4 and line a baking tray with wax/greaseproof paper. Prepare the glaze by whisking the milk and confectioner's/icing sugar together until completely smooth.

When the dough is ready, divide it into four. Roll each portion out into a rectangle about 2½in × 4½in/6cm × 12cm. Spread a quarter of the filling down the center of each dough sheet in a sausage shape. Carefully fold one side of the dough over the filling, then fold over the other, gently pinching where the dough meets to seal. Flip the cookie log seam-side down and, with a sharp knife, cut parallel chunks 1½–2in/4–5cm thick.

Place on the baking tray, seam-side down, brush with the glaze, sprinkle with sesame seeds, and bake for 20–25 minutes until the tops are golden.

Leave to cool completely on a wire rack, then store in an airtight container.

Lumi are sundried limes used in Persian and Gulf cuisine to add a tangy sourness to rice dishes and stews. Crushing the lumi and letting it infuse in boiling water makes for a warming and highly digestible winter tea. In stews, the lumi softens, oozing a thick, tangy syrup that cuts through rich sauces. In the Middle East, ground lumi powder is often used to marinate meat and perfume desserts. If you can't find lumi, use fresh lime juice and zest instead.

LUMI DATE SLICE

MAKES 10–15 SLICES

8oz/220g dates, roughly chopped

4oz/100g dried shredded/ desiccated coconut

⅔ cup/4oz/100g jumbo rolled oats

3 tbsp self-rising flour

9 tbsp/4½oz/120g butter

¼ cup/2oz/50g light brown sugar

3 tbsp golden syrup

1 lumi, grated, or juice and zest 1 lime

Preheat the oven to 340F/175C/gas 4. Grease and line a 9in/23cm square cake pan.

Soak the chopped dates in scant ½ cup/100ml of boiling water and set aside. Put the coconut, oats, and flour in a large bowl.

Melt the butter and sugar together, stirring until combined. Pour over the dry ingredients and stir using a large metal spoon. Drain the dates and add them to the mixture. Pour in the golden syrup and add the grated lumi or the lime zest and juice, depending on what you're using. Give everything a very good stir—the mixture will be thick.

Pour the mixture into the cake pan and, with a spatula or damp spoon, smooth out into the four corners of the pan. Bake for 25–30 minutes until golden brown on top.

Remove from the oven and leave to cool completely on a wire rack before slicing into chunky squares.

It is said of dates: Astrologers have given them to Mars, perhaps to please the lady Venus with

William Westmacott, **A Scripture Herbal**, 1695

On my way to Liwa's yearly date festival, I stopped off for *macarons* at the Dubai branch of chic Parisian café Ladurée. In France, their shops offer a kaleidoscope of brightly-colored *macarons*—71 flavors to be precise. A dozen of the most popular were rolled out across the Gulf, including a date *parfum*, a magenta cookie enclosing a date and fig ganache. In my kitchen, I set about making them in all colors and flavors and found they were easy, fun, and relatively quick to make—not to mention inexpensive (especially compared to the bought version!) In the end, the subtle licorice-tasting fennel shells and the date cream filling with its fresh mint ribbon got along the best. I love this humorous French date reference: in 1923 J Manchon wrote *Le Slang*, a dictionary of slang and unconventional English, and listed the phrase *You date! Que tu es drole!*

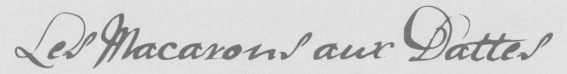

FENNEL MACARONS WITH FRESH MINT DATE GANACHE

MAKES 15 MACARONS

3oz/80g ground almonds

1 cup/4oz/110g confectioner's/icing sugar

1 tsp fennel seeds

2 large egg whites

2 tbsp/1oz/25g fine raw/golden caster sugar

For the filling

4oz/100g cream cheese

2½oz/75g dates, finely chopped

1 tbsp date syrup

1 tbsp finely chopped fresh mint

You will also need a pastry/piping bag with a ½in/1cm tip.

Sift the ground almonds and confectioner's/icing sugar into a large bowl. Grind the fennel seeds using a mortar and pestle, discard any husks, and add to the almonds and sugar.

In another bowl, whisk the egg whites until they form soft peaks, then gradually add the sugar in three stages, whisking continually until the sugar has been absorbed and the mixture is stiff and glossy.

Using a large metal spoon, gently fold the almond mixture into the egg whites until well combined. The mixture should be slightly looser but dry.

Line a baking tray with wax/greaseproof paper. Spoon the mixture into the pastry/piping bag and start by dabbing a tiny amount underneath the paper, in all four corners, to prevent it from sliding. Pipe out 30 small discs 1in/3cm wide onto the baking tray. Once they have all been piped, lift and drop the tray twice on the work surface to get any air out of the shells. Leave to stand for 30 minutes at room temperature until a thin skin forms on each of the shells.

Preheat the oven to 320F/160C/gas 3. Bake for 10–12 minutes with the oven door slightly ajar until set and pale golden. Leave to cool completely on a wire rack.

Meanwhile, gently beat the cream cheese, dates, and date syrup together until creamy. Stir in the fresh mint.

Pipe (or spoon) the ganache between two equally-sized *macaron* shells and press together very lightly to sandwich the filling. Refrigerate to set or eat immediately.

In 1596, Thomas Dawson published *The Good Huyswifes Jewell*, a cookbook aimed at the wives of newly-rich merchants in Elizabethan England. It contained recipes for custards, pies, and "all things necessary for a banquet." What's more, the very first recipe for a trifle—that quintessential English layered confection of cream, fruit, and biscuits—and over 25 dishes with dates: like *mutton and veale pie, spinnach and date fritters, leg of mutton with a pudding, bake meates,* and *stewe of cocke*. Dates were added as a sweetener, but also to thicken custards and pies. This recipe, while very much of our time, is reminiscent of Dawson's 16th-century date recipe for "another pretie dishe, with dates, and the juice of two or three orenges."

The orange and date duo is very festive. My friend Laszlo, who grew up in Germany, remembers being given an orange and a date as a treat every Christmas. In fact, up until the 18th century, most Christmas trees were adorned with goodies like apples, nuts, and dates.

ORANGE, DATE, AND CINNAMON MUFFINS

MAKES 12 MUFFINS

1 orange

1 large egg

5 tbsp/2½oz/75g butter

6oz/170g dates

½ cup/125ml milk

1 tbsp honey

1⅓ cups/6½oz/185g all-purpose/plain flour

1 tsp baking powder

1 tsp baking soda/bicarbonate of soda

1½ tsp cinnamon

⅓ cup/3oz/80g brown sugar

Preheat the oven to 400F/200C/gas 6. Line a 12-hole muffin pan with paper baking cups/cases.

Slice the orange into quarters and remove any seeds, but leave the peel on. In a food processor, whizz the orange, egg, butter, dates, milk, and honey together until finely chopped and well combined.

Sift the flour, baking powder, baking soda, cinnamon, and a pinch of salt into a large bowl, then add the sugar. Make a well in the center and pour in the date and orange mixture, stirring until just combined. The mixture will be runny.

Spoon into the baking cups/cases, filling each about three-quarters full. Bake for 15–20 minutes until risen and golden brown.

Remove from the oven and leave to cool in the pan for 15 minutes before transferring to a wire rack to cool completely.

Liwa

The Liwa Oasis is a green belt of villages and date plantations on the edge of the Empty Quarter desert, in the UAE. Each year the area hosts a week-long date festival during the harvest season in July, celebrating all things date-related. Thousands of visitors converge for this annual event where local farmers proudly display their crops to compete for cash prizes. Date honey, ice cream, and fresh juice can be sampled and bought, palm frond houses visited, and the handmade palm baskets woven by the women of Liwa purchased.

مهرجان ليوا للرطب
Liwa Date Festival

مهرجان ليوا للرطب
Liwa Date Festival

المركز الأول

1st Place

Maamoul are shortbread cookies with a pistachio, date, or walnut paste filling. They are quintessentially Levantine. Locals in Beirut and Damascus wink and whisper when they discuss their *maamoul* suppliers, such is the competition. Some *maamoul* recipes call for all-purpose/plain flour, but the grainy, crumbly texture of the semolina is the trademark of this cookie. A box of these always contains three shapes: oblong for pistachio, round for dates, and domed for walnuts. Moni, a great Beiruti home cook, inspired these.

Moni's Maamoul

DATE SHORTBREADS

MAKES 20 COOKIES

¾ cup/5½oz/150g semolina

½ cup/2½oz/75g all-purpose/plain flour

¼ tsp baking powder

1 tbsp superfine/caster sugar

5 tbsp/2½oz/75g butter, melted and cooled slightly

1 tbsp rose water

1 tsp orange blossom water

For the filling

4oz/100g dates, finely chopped

1–2 tsp vegetable oil

In a large bowl, mix the semolina, flour, baking powder, sugar, and a pinch of salt together. Pour in the melted butter and the rose and orange blossom waters. With your fingers, work the butter and waters into the flour until fully incorporated. Add a tablespoon or two of water, or enough to bind the mixture into a semi-wet dough. Shape the dough into a round ball—it should feel grainy but pliable. Cover and chill overnight.

Remove the dough from the fridge and return to room temperature. If the dough is still very hard, wet your fingers with a little water or milk and work it until softened. Break off walnut-sized pieces of dough and roll between your palms to form a ball—you should get about 20 balls.

For the filling, mash up the dates with the oil to a soft paste. This can also be done using a food processor. Roll into small date balls as many as you have dough balls, but about half the size.

Preheat the oven to 350F/180C/gas 4 and line a baking tray with wax/greaseproof paper.

To assemble the cookies, place a dough ball in your palm. With the thumb and index fingers of your other hand, make an indentation in the center, working your way around to an even thickness. Insert a date ball, then pinch and press the dough to seal it around the filling. Roll the filled ball between your palms to smooth out. Transfer to a baking tray seam-side down and flatten slightly with your palm. Repeat with the remaining dough balls.

Decorate the top of each cookie with a crisscross pattern using a butter knife or use a *maamoul* mold: insert a filled cookie, gently press down, then knock out.

Bake for 20–25 minutes; they're done when the tops are pale and the bottoms are golden. Cool on a wire rack. These keep for weeks.

In the Philippines, dates were once so costly that a traditional butterscotch brownie with dates and walnuts (a blondie) was called "food for the gods." This indulgent brownie recipe of dates, dark chocolate, and ruby-red berries could also be fit for otherworldly royalty. I limited the quantity of sugar, but even so, each square is indulgent, decadent, and should be uninhibitedly enjoyed as the delicious aroma fills the kitchen. If you can't get hold of dried cranberries, use any sour berries or cherries of your choice. In a nod to my Middle Eastern roots, I also tested these with *zereshk*, tiny barberries used to bejewel Persian rice. Tart and sour, they produced a batch of perfectly sweet and sour brownies.

Best Chocoberry Brownies

CRANBERRY AND DATE BROWNIES

**MAKES UP TO
20 BROWNIES**

5½oz/150g dates, roughly chopped

1oz/25g cranberries, dried sour cherries, or barberries (*zereshk*)

2 tbsp date syrup

16 tbsp/8oz/225g butter

5½oz/150g best-quality dark chocolate, chopped

2oz/50g white chocolate, chopped

5 large eggs, at room temperature

½ cup/4oz/100g light brown sugar

1 cup/5oz/140g all-purpose/plain flour

⅓ cup/1½oz/30g best-quality cocoa powder

Preheat the oven to 350F/180C/gas 4. Lightly grease and line an 8in/20cm square cake pan.

Put the dates, berries, and date syrup into a small bowl. Stir well to combine and set aside to soak.

Set a heatproof bowl over a pan of simmering water, then tip in the butter and chocolates, stirring occasionally until melted and smooth. Remove from the heat and leave to cool slightly.

Using an electric mixer, beat the eggs and sugar together in a large bowl until doubled in volume. Pour in the melted chocolate and beat briefly until combined. Sift in the flour, cocoa, and a pinch of salt, then tip in the soaked fruit. Fold into the egg mixture using a large metal spoon. Pour into the pan, level, and spread to the four corners of the pan.

Bake for 25 minutes until the top is shiny and set, the sides have come away slightly from the edge of the pan, and the center feels springy and slightly wobbly. In this case, a skewer inserted into the center should not come out clean!

Remove from the oven and leave to cool in the pan before lifting out and slicing into chunky squares. Ideally eat warm, with a scoop of vanilla ice cream or dollop of whipped cream, or place in an airtight container to be equally enjoyed at room temperature later.

Oats are a natural partner to dates, and a loyal friend to cinnamon and brown sugar. These old-fashioned drop cookies wow in their simplicity and deliciousness. My sister and her kids love to make them and they're perfect snacks for any date or wholegrain lovers. The dough can also be made ahead and frozen, then thawed just before use. This was the first recipe I tested for the book, suggested to me by Razan, a keen baker and great friend.

DATE AND OATMEAL COOKIES

MAKES 36 COOKIES

12 tbsp/6oz/175g butter, softened

1 cup/7oz/200g light brown sugar

3 large eggs, at room temperature

1 tsp vanilla extract

1⅓ cups/6½oz/190g all-purpose/plain flour

1 tsp baking powder

2 tsp cinnamon

½ tsp baking soda/bicarbonate of soda

7oz/200g dates, roughly chopped

scant 1 cup/5oz/140g oats

Preheat the oven to 350F/180C/gas 4 and line a baking sheet with wax/greaseproof paper.

In a large bowl, beat the butter and sugar together with an electric mixer until pale and creamy. Add the eggs one at a time, beating well after each, then stir in the vanilla.

Sift the flour, baking powder, cinnamon, baking soda/bicarbonate of soda, and a pinch of salt into the batter, then fold in. Tip in the dates and oats and stir well to combine. The dough should be soft but sticky.

Using a teaspoon, drop the dough onto the baking sheet, leaving about 2in/5cm between each cookie.

Bake for 8–12 minutes or until lightly golden and brown around the edges. Leave to cool on a wire rack.

Lady Capulet: Hold, take these keys, and fetch more spices, nurse
Nurse: They call for dates and quinces in the pastry

William Shakespeare, **Romeo and Juliet**, Scene 4, Act 4

Pinwheels always look impressive, despite how easy they are to make. Their bright, nutty filling makes them look so pretty and taste delicious, too. These have a lovely crumbly texture and the dough can be made ahead, then frozen until ready to bake. If pressed, I would serve them with vanilla ice cream, but really, they are perfect just as they are.

PINWHEEL DATE SHORTBREADS

MAKES 25–30 COOKIES

2 cups/9oz/250g all-purpose/plain flour, plus extra for dusting

⅓ cup/2½oz/75g superfine raw/golden caster sugar

zest ½ lemon

11 tbsp/5½oz/150g unsalted butter, chilled and cubed

1 large egg, lightly beaten

2 tbsp runny honey, for glazing

For the filling

9oz/250g dates

4oz/100g pistachios

zest and juice ½ lemon

Mix the flour, sugar, and lemon zest together in a large bowl. Add the butter and rub it in using your fingertips until the mixture resembles breadcrumbs. Pour in the beaten egg and bring it together to form a dough. Cover and chill for 30 minutes. Meanwhile, whizz all of the ingredients for the filling together in a food processor until finely chopped.

Preheat the oven to 365F/190C/gas 5 and line a baking tray with wax/greaseproof paper.

On a lightly floured surface, roll the dough out to a 12in × 8in/30cm × 20cm rectangle about ¼in/½cm thick. Spread the date and nut mixture evenly over the dough sheet, leaving a gap along the long edges. Roll the side nearest you away and towards the other end, into a long log. Use a palette knife to help you roll and don't worry about cracks appearing, just patch them up as you go.

Slice the log into ¼in/½cm thick cookies, then transfer them to the baking tray. Flatten them slightly with your palm, then bake for 12–15 minutes until pale golden.

Remove from the oven, brush each lightly with the honey, then transfer to a wire rack to finish cooling completely.

Date cakes

The medjool is known as the king of dates: large, fleshy, and sweet, with irresistible toffee notes. This dessert is at the heart of this book, a classic date-flecked English dessert consisting of a moist sponge cake enrobed in a luscious, caramely sauce. You can't help but imagine it being eaten at sumptuous banquets hundreds of years ago—but in fact the dessert first appeared on menus in the 20th century. Although much contested, the town of Cartmel in gastronomic Cumbria, England, today lays claim to being "home of the sticky toffee pudding." Already known for its 12th-century priory, the village has achieved worldwide fame for its gorgeously gooey desserts, handmade in the local village shop. If you're tempted to make just one dessert from this book, make this the one.

King-of-Dates Pudding

STICKY SPONGE CAKE WITH A TOFFEE SAUCE

SERVES 6–8

7oz/200g medjool dates, pitted and roughly chopped

1 tsp baking soda/bicarbonate of soda

5 tbsp/2½oz/60g butter, softened

½ cup/4½oz/120g soft dark brown sugar

2 tbsp golden syrup

2 large eggs, at room temperature

1 tsp vanilla extract

1¼ cups/6oz/180g all-purpose/plain flour

1 tsp baking powder

For the toffee sauce

½ cup/4½oz/120g light brown sugar

2 tbsp date syrup (optional)

8 tbsp/4oz/100g unsalted butter

scant 1 cup/7fl oz/200ml extra-heavy/double cream

Put the dates and baking soda/bicarbonate of soda in a small bowl. Cover with a scant 1 cup/200ml of boiling water, stir, then leave to soak for 30 minutes. When cool, blitz the mixture to a purée in a food processor and set aside.

Preheat the oven to 325F/170C/gas 5. Grease and line a 7in/18cm square baking pan.

In a large bowl, beat the butter, sugar, and golden syrup together until light and creamy. Add the eggs and vanilla, then fold in the date purée and mix well. Put the flour and baking powder into another large bowl, tip in the date mixture, and give everything a good stir.

Pour into the baking pan and bake for 20–25 minutes until firm but springy. The cake should feel a little bouncy when you touch it, and a skewer inserted into the center should come out clean. If you're not serving immediately, let it cool completely, then refrigerate.

Just before serving, prepare the toffee sauce. Place all the ingredients in a saucepan and cook over a medium heat for a few minutes, whisking continuously until the sauce thickens. Sieve to remove any sugar stones.

When the cake has finished baking (or reheating), remove it from the pan, prick the top in several places with a skewer, and pour on the toffee sauce. Slice into squares and serve warm with custard or cream.

Cartmel

In Cumbria sits the pretty hamlet of Cartmel, famous for it's derby horse race and it's village shop, the home of sticky toffee pudding. Once a small family operation, today a nearby factory packs enough dates into it's luscious puddings to meet national (and international) demand. Banana and ginger are runner-up flavors to the favorite, traditional toffee sauce. In recent years the village has become a culinary hub with a michelin-starred restaurant and gastropubs, a sweet place to stop after a day's hike in the green hills above.

My good friend Monica and her charming cousins Antoine and Georg came to dinner one summer. Years before, the brothers had owned a successful bakery in Melbourne, where cakes such as this were their trademark: they generously shared this recipe. Curious to trace the name, I discovered a strong connection between Canada, its outdoor culture, and its historic link to Britain. During World War II, the lumberjack's twin appeared in England as Queen Elizabeth cake, named after the Queen Mother, a much-loved figure during the war, when the cake was sold to raise funds. Even today, anyone using the recipe is asked to make a charitable donation—as I hope you will. A crown of crunchy coconut makes it fit for a sweet-toothed queen.

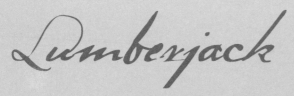

QUEEN ELIZABETH CAKE

SERVES 8–10

2 apples, cored and grated

9oz/250g dates, roughly chopped

1 tsp baking soda/bicarbonate of soda

9 tbsp/4½oz/125g butter, softened

¾ cup/7oz/200g brown sugar

2 large eggs, lightly beaten

1 tsp vanilla extract

1⅔ cup/8oz/225g all-purpose/plain flour

1 tsp baking powder

For the topping

4½oz/125g dried shredded/desiccated coconut

¼ cup/2oz/50g brown sugar

1 large egg, lightly beaten

Preheat the oven to 350F/180C/gas 4. Grease and line a 9in/23cm springform cake pan.

Place the apples, dates, and baking soda/bicarbonate of soda in a bowl, then pour over 1 cup/250ml of boiling water.

Beat the butter and sugar together until light and creamy. Add the eggs and vanilla and mix well. Pour in the soaked apple-date mixture, then fold in the flour and baking powder until everything is well combined.

Pour into the cake pan and bake for 40–45 minutes until a skewer inserted into the center comes out clean.

Just before the cake is ready, make the topping. Place the coconut and sugar in a saucepan over a medium heat and stir continuously until the sugar has dissolved. Add the lightly beaten egg and mix well.

Once the cake is cooked, remove it from the oven and pour over the coconut topping. Smooth with the back of a spoon, then return the cake to the oven for a further 10–15 minutes until the topping is golden and set.

Leave to cool in the pan for a few minutes, then transfer to a wire rack to finish cooling completely.

Not long ago, ancient writing tablets from 1700BC were discovered in present-day Iraq, containing the oldest recipes known to man. This is how we came to know what the Babylonians ate for breakfast and what they offered their gods in the temples. They used date syrup to sweeten food, referring to it as honey, and also enjoyed dates dried and in a fermented beverage. Palace cake was made in honor of the gods who were worshipped in the temples of Ur on the banks of the Euphrates. It contained raisins, aniseed, and an unbelievable amount of fat and dates. The original recipe mentions "oodles of butter" and vine leaves to line the baking dish—Babylonian wax/greaseproof paper, of sorts. This lightened version, with pineapple and date slices arranged in a sunny pattern, is delicious and far more digestible.

Upside-down in Babylon

PINEAPPLE PALACE CAKE

SERVES 6

8 tbsp/4oz/100g butter

½ cup/4oz/100g fine raw/golden caster sugar

2 large eggs

1 tsp vanilla extract

⅔ cup/4oz/100g self-rising flour

1 tsp baking powder

2 tbsp runny honey, for glazing

For the caramel topping

4 tbsp/2oz/60g butter

¼ cup/2oz/60g light brown sugar

8 medjool dates, sliced in half lengthways

4 pineapple rings from a can, drained and chopped

Preheat the oven to 375F/190C/gas 5. Grease an 8in/20cm tarte tatin pan or round cake pan.

To make the caramel topping (which will be baked as the base), put the butter and brown sugar in a saucepan over medium heat. Stir continuously until the sugar has dissolved and started to bubble at the sides. Pour the syrup into the pan and swirl to coat the base. Arrange the dates in a circular pattern, cut-side up. Do the same with the pineapple, placing chunks between each date.

Beat the butter and sugar together in a large bowl until light and creamy. Gradually add the eggs and vanilla, fold in the flour and baking powder, and mix well to combine. Spoon the mixture into the pan over the fruit, smoothing with the back of a spoon to ensure all the fruit is covered.

Bake for 25–30 minutes until risen, golden, and a skewer inserted into the center of the cake comes out clean. Leave to cool in the pan for 5 minutes before inverting onto a serving plate and glazing the top with the honey. Serve warm.

A traditional shortcrust pastry requires working and lengthy resting. This simple, sugar- and dairy-free tart base doesn't need time to rest, is easy to work, *and* tastes great. Use one or all of the nuts listed—any combination will work with the dates. For the fruit topping, contrast the caramel-hued crust with vibrant summer berries or exotic mangos, kiwis, and pomegranate seeds. Baking the bases first firms them up a little, and brings out the nutty flavors, but you can enjoy them raw, too. Either way, they taste amazing and are impressive to serve up.

Feel-good Summer Tarts

DATE AND BERRY TARTLETS

MAKES 4 SMALL TARTS

5½oz/150g mixture of hazelnuts, cashews, or almonds

7oz/200g dates, chopped

flour, for dusting

fresh berries or sliced fruit, to finish

For the Filling

½ cup/4oz/100g mascarpone

⅓ cup/2½oz/75g yogurt

zest and juice 1 lemon or lime

2 tbsp confectioner's/icing sugar

Preheat the oven to 345F/170C/gas 4. Lightly butter 4 fluted tart pans.

Scatter the nuts on a baking tray and toast for 8–10 minutes, with a few shakes in between, until aromatic and lightly golden. Set aside and leave to cool slightly.

Using a food processor, whizz the nuts and dates until finely chopped and fully combined. Tip out onto a lightly floured surface and roll the date pastry into discs slightly larger than your pans. Carefully drape the discs over your tart pans, pressing the date pastry into the edges and trim off any excess pastry.

If you're baking the pastry, bake for 10–12 minutes until firm, golden brown, and crisp. Leave to cool completely before filling.

For the filling, whip all the ingredients together and spoon into the tart bases. Decorate with berries or sliced fruit of your choice.

Roman soldiers battling the mighty Persians used to eat fruit-and-nut cakes called satura. Their encounter with the date fruit is vividly drawn in the 1852 book, *History of Greece*, as the soldiers enter Greek villages "for provisions and find large quantities of corn, dates of such beauty, freshness and size and flavor—wine and vinegar also made from date palm." Then as now, dates have delighted and provided sustenance. In present-day Italy, this variation on the crumbly Italian classic with its rustic flavors and golden hue is pure alchemy: the dates lend a smooth, caramel sweetness, the pomegranate topping makes this a visually stunning ruby-red treat. It also stores well so you can keep enjoying it for days.

Ruby Polenta Cake

DATE AND POLENTA CAKE WITH POMEGRANATE SYRUP

SERVES 8–10

7oz/200g dates, roughly chopped

8 tbsp/4oz/100g butter, softened

¾ cup/5½oz/150g fine raw/golden caster sugar

2 large eggs

9 oz/250g ricotta

½ cup/4fl oz/125ml skim milk

1¼ cups/7oz/200g polenta

1¼ cups/6oz/175g self-rising flour

1 heaped tsp baking powder

4oz/100g pomegranate seeds

For the Pomegranate Syrup

1¼ cups/10fl oz/300ml pomegranate juice

2 tbsp pomegranate molasses

1 tbsp fine raw/golden caster sugar

2oz/50g dates, sliced lengthways

Preheat the oven to 320F/160C/gas 3. Grease and line a 9in/22cm springform cake pan.

Put the dates in a small bowl and pour over a scant 1 cup/200ml boiling water. Leave to soak for 20 minutes or so.

Meanwhile, beat the butter and sugar together in a large bowl until light and creamy. Add the eggs one at a time, whisking well after each addition, then stir in the ricotta and milk.

Drain the dates from their liquid and fold them into the mixture. Sift the polenta, flour, and baking powder into the mixture, then fold in thoroughly until smooth.

Pour into the pan and bake for 50–60 minutes until risen and a skewer inserted into the center comes out clean. The center should still feel springy.

Meanwhile, make the topping. Put the juice, molasses, and sugar into a saucepan and cook over low heat, stirring constantly, until the sugar has dissolved. Turn up the heat and boil rapidly until the mixture has reduced by two thirds, then stir in the sliced dates and set aside to cool.

As soon as the cake is ready, remove it from the oven and poke it with a skewer a few times. Pour most of the syrup and dates over the cake, reserving a little of the syrup for serving.

Sprinkle liberally with pomegranate seeds and serve warm or at room temperature, drizzled with the remaining syrup.

They say there's a cheesecake for every occasion. This baked version, with its silky, creamy date interior, is a dream—it is also low on sugar. Enveloping dates in cream cheese delivers magical vanilla and honey tones, not unlike those of the celebrated Barhi, known as the honey date. This all-American baked cheesecake had to be named after Coachella, California's date-producing valley, where a music festival amid the towering date palms has become the area's biggest yearly draw. I've kept to the traditional crumbly base but you could up the date ante by mixing chopped dates with the crackers/ biscuits for a gloriously sticky, rich base. Pleases on so many levels.

Sun-baked Coachella

VANILLA AND DATE CHEESECAKE

SERVES 6–8

7oz/200g dates

9oz/250g graham crackers or digestive biscuits

5 tbsp/2½oz/120g butter, melted

11oz/300g full-fat cream cheese, at room temperature

¼ cup/2oz/50g fine raw/golden caster sugar

1 tbsp cornstarch/cornflour

2 large eggs, beaten

1 cup/9fl oz/250ml extra-heavy/ double cream

1 tsp vanilla extract

Line a 9in/22cm springform cake pan with wax/greaseproof paper.

Soak the dates in ½ cup/125ml boiling water for 20 minutes.

Bash the crackers/biscuits in a small plastic bag with a rolling pin until crushed, then beat together with the butter until fully combined. Alternatively, you can whizz them together in a food processor. Press the crumb base evenly into the bottom of the pan with your fingers or the back of a spoon. Chill the base in the fridge for 30 minutes or so to firm up.

Preheat the oven to 350F/180C/gas 4.

Tip the dates and soaking water into the bowl of a food processor, then gradually add the cream cheese, sugar, and cornstarch/cornflour, whizzing together until the dates are finely chopped and the mixture is smooth. Add the beaten eggs, cream, and vanilla and beat together again until combined.

Pour over the chilled base, evening out the surface with a tilt or two. Bake for 40–45 minutes until the edges have set and the top of the cheesecake is pale and lightly golden, with the side coming away from the pan.

Turn the oven off and leave the cheesecake to cool in the oven. Once completely cool, place in the fridge for at least two hours until set. When ready to serve, bring back to room temperature or serve chilled.

Coachella Valley

Since the 1920s, the Coachella Valley has been home of the date palm in North America. A short drive from Palm Springs, California, along Highway 111, the town of Indio sits at the heart of date-land and is host to the National Date Festival every February. An institution on the "date strip," no visit is complete without a stop at Shields date garden, where a giant knight orders you inside. A quirky 15-minute presentation on the Romance and Sex Life of the Date, playing here since the 1950s, sets the mood as the garden's signature "blonde" and "brunette" dates are sampled and a deliciously refreshing date shake is enjoyed. Here date harvest season starts in September, a few months after the Gulf's.

The deglet noor is North Africa's other grande dame date, alongside the medjool, a native of the oases of Tunisia and Algeria. Legend has it that it was named after Lalla Noor, a poor local saint who made a rosary from date seeds to recite God's 99 names with everyday. When she died, the Saharan villagers buried her on the spot with the rosary, from which sprung 99 palms yielding excellent dates, which people called *deglet noora* or Noora's seedlings. This see-through date is also known as "the translucent;" in Arabic, *noor* means light. Not long ago at a long, lazy lunch I enjoyed a delicious North-African-inspired date and prune torte enrobed in smooth chocolate, not unlike this one.

Decadent Chocolate Torte

FLOURLESS HAZELNUT, DATE, AND PRUNE CAKE

SERVES 8–10

4 large eggs, separated

½ tsp vanilla extract

scant ½ cup/3oz/85g light brown sugar

6oz/175g hazelnuts or almonds

4½oz/120g dates, roughly chopped

4oz/100g prunes, roughly chopped

4oz/100g plain chocolate, finely chopped

Preheat the oven to 345F/175C/gas 4. Grease and line a 9in/22cm springform cake pan.

Lightly whisk the egg yolks with the vanilla extract in a small bowl until light and creamy. In a large bowl, whisk the egg whites with a pinch of salt until foamy. Add half the sugar and whisk until pale and stiff peaks form. In a food processor, whizz the nuts with the remaining sugar until crumb-like but not too fine.

Using a large metal spoon, fold the egg yolk mixture into the whites. Add the nuts, fruit, and chocolate, then fold together until combined.

Pour into the cake pan and bake for 20 minutes or until the top is set and pale golden. Turn the oven off and, with the door ajar, leave the torte to cool completely before removing.

Enjoy warm. A slice will reveal the fondant goodness within.

In Europe back in the 1700s, people ate dense fruitcake made of fruit and nuts to mark the annual nut harvest around the winter solstice. Today, garden vegetables like squash, beets, zucchini/courgettes, and parsnips are also great in baking, and inspired this fresh, moist cake. It's a cross between a carrot and banana cake, a fresh-tasting but not-too-sweet loaf. I love the way the warm colors blend and the apricots gleam when you slice into it. This is a cake you can eat without regret, packed with textured, finely grated vegetables and fruit, and using dark brown sugar to give it a rich, molasses flavor without that sugary hit. Perfect in the mornings or afternoons with a cup of tea. Dairy-free, it keeps longer than most cakes.

Golden Fruit Trio

SWEET POTATO, APRICOT, AND DATE LOAF

SERVES 8–10

1 cup/5oz/150g all-purpose/plain flour

2oz/50g ground almonds

1 tsp pumpkin pie/mixed spice

1 tsp baking soda/bicarbonate of soda

⅔ cup/5oz/150g dark brown sugar

⅔ cup/5fl oz/150ml sunflower oil

3 large eggs

6oz/175g sweet potato, grated

5oz/150g dates, roughly chopped

2oz/50g soft apricots, roughly chopped

2½oz/75g pecans, finely chopped

Preheat the oven to 320F/160C/gas 3. Grease and line a 2lb/900g loaf pan.

Put the flour, ground almonds, spice, baking soda/bicarbonate of soda, and a pinch of salt in a large bowl, then mix together well.

Beat the sugar and oil together with an electric mixer until more or less combined. Don't worry if there are the odd lumps of sugar. Gradually add the eggs, beating well after each addition, until the mixture is thick and amber colored. Fold in the flour mixture with a large metal spoon, then add the sweet potato, fruit, and nuts and mix together well.

Pour into the loaf pan and bake for about 1–1¼ hours until golden, risen, and firm to the touch and a skewer inserted into the center comes out clean. As the dark sugar caramelizes, the top could look wet despite the cake being cooked, so keep an eye on it as it approaches the 1-hour mark.

Leave in the pan for 10 minutes, then turn out and leave to cool completely on a wire rack.

Date syrup has the texture of molasses and the flavor of treacle and deep caramel. It is a whole food, made with nothing but dates, boiled and softened to a syrup. It is a delicious alternative to sugars, maple syrup, or honey. Tahini is a sesame seed paste popularly blended with chickpeas, garlic, and lemon juice to make hummus, the iconic Mediterranean dip. It looks like a paler, more liquified peanut butter. Versatile and nutritious, tahini is used in many cuisines and pairs equally well with sweet and savory. In this sumptuous chocolate and date cake, the tahini topping lends a creamy nuttiness and a touch of glamor. An elegant, dressy cake that won't fail to impress.

Black and White Delight

CHOCOLATE DATE CAKE WITH TAHINI AND WHITE CHOCOLATE SAUCE

SERVES 8

7oz/200g dates, chopped

14 tbsp/7oz/200g butter

12oz/350g dark chocolate (maximum 70% cocoa solids)

2 tbsp date syrup

5 large eggs, separated

½ cup/4oz/100g light brown sugar

4oz/100g ground almonds

For the sauce

5 tbsp tahini

7oz/200g white chocolate

scant ½ cup/4fl oz/100ml extra-heavy/double cream (optional)

Preheat the oven to 345F/170C/gas 4. Grease and line a 9in/23cm springform cake pan.

Put the dates, butter, chocolate, and date syrup in a bowl set over a pan of barely simmering water. Stir once or twice until melted and combined. Set aside to cool slightly.

In another bowl, beat the egg yolks with the sugar until pale and creamy. Pour in the chocolate and date mixture, then stir until incorporated. Sift the ground almonds into the mixture and stir well to combine. Whisk the egg whites until they start to form stiff peaks, then fold carefully, and completely, into the mixture, using a large metal spoon.

Pour into the cake pan and bake for 45–50 minutes or until a skewer inserted into the center comes out clean.

Meanwhile, make the sauce. Melt the tahini and white chocolate in a bowl set over a pan of barely simmering water. Remove from the heat. For a thicker ganache, stir in the cream.

Plate up the cake and pour the sauce generously over each slice, ideally while still warm.

Puddings, fudges, and custards

From the 15th century, dates, prunes, and raisins were traded West to bejewel the dishes and banquets of Europe's gourmand nobility. They were hugely expensive and, along with prized spices like nutmeg, saffron, vanilla, and cinnamon, were used to flavor cooked dishes and baked into cakes, especially at Christmas time. The *Boke of Kokery*, an English cookbook from the 1440s, contains countless medieval recipes using dates and one particular custard "made with dates, eggs and good creame." Up until the 19th century, a custard was an open-faced pie of crust with a fruit or meat filling and a cream topping. This is an adapted recipe.

To make a Custard, breake your egges into a bowle, and put your creame into another bowle, and straine your egges into the creame, and put in saffron, cloves and mace, and a little synamon and ginger, and if you will some suger and butter, and season it with salte, and melte your butter, and stirre it with the ladle a good while, and dubbe your custard with dates or currans.

DATE AND SAFFRON CUSTARD, c.1440

MAKES 2½ CUPS/600ML CUSTARD

scant 1 cup/7fl oz/200ml milk

large pinch saffron

¼ tsp ground cloves

½ tsp cinnamon

½ tsp ground ginger

scant 1 cup/7fl oz/200ml extra-heavy/double cream

4 large egg yolks

⅓ cup/2½oz/75g superfine/caster sugar

2 tsp cornstarch/cornflour

Pour the milk into a saucepan and mix in the spices. Leave to stand for ten minutes until the spices have infused the milk.

Pour in the cream, then gently bring to boiling point. Remove from the heat and leave to cool slightly.

Meanwhile, beat the eggs yolks with the sugar and cornstarch/cornflour until pale, then pour over the hot milk, whisking continuously. Tip into a clean saucepan and heat gently until thickened.

Serve with date slices or pour over the Date and Plum crumble (p. 108).

Indian restaurants often serve *payasam* or *kheer*, a South Asian rice pudding popular at festivals and on special occasions. This version has Ayurvedic properties: it's sugar-free, full of magnesium-rich cashews and liver-cleansing dates to balance the *doshas*, the body's energy centers. Ayurveda is a traditional Hindu system of medicine based on the idea that eating certain foods and spices leads to optimal mental and physical health. Ayurvedic date and coconut balls and date shakes made of milk, dates, raisins, cashews, almonds, rosewater, and saffron are also considered to be the ultimate healthy pick-me-ups.

Perfumed Payasam

ROSE WATER, DATE, AND CASHEW PUDDING

SERVES 4–6

2½ cups/20fl oz/600ml skim milk

pinch saffron threads

5½oz/150g dates, roughly chopped

4oz/100g cashews

1 tsp rose water

3 tablespoons/1oz/30g cornstarch/cornflour

2oz/50g pistachios, chopped, to serve

Pour the milk into a saucepan and add the saffron, dates, and nuts. Bring to a boil over low-medium heat and simmer with the lid on for about 10 minutes until the dates and nuts have softened. In a food processor, blend together until the dates are tiny brown specks. Return to the pan, add the rose water, and bring to a boil again, simmering gently. Keep stirring the mixture as it can easily catch.

Mix the cornstarch/cornflour with just enough water to make a paste, then pour it into the simmering mixture. Stir constantly for 2 minutes until the mixture thickens to an oatmeal/porridge consistency.

Remove from the heat and transfer to glass cups or bowls, filling each one three quarters full. Leave to cool, then refrigerate until ready to eat. Sprinkle with the chopped pistachios to serve.

Fruit-filled crumbles are synonymous with England, but the bubbling mass of fruit and textured, buttery crumble is popular in many countries. In Newfoundland, Canada, for example, a date crumble is a popular snack, packed into bars and rolled in coconut and brown sugar. For this recipe, I experimented with some of my favorite fruits: apples, nectarines, and pears but finally settled on plums. They lend a gorgeous autumnal feel and are delicious alongside the dates, in a luscious palette of deep magenta and purple. I like adding flaked almonds to the topping for just that extra bit of crunch and goodness.

DATE AND PLUM CRUMBLE

SERVES 4–6

5oz/150g dates, roughly chopped

6 plums, pitted and quartered

juice ½ a lemon

1 tsp cinnamon

¼ tsp pumpkin pie/mixed spice

2 tbsp date syrup

For the crumble topping

scant 1½ cups/7oz/200g all-purpose/plain flour

12 tbsp/6oz/180g butter, chilled and diced

⅓ cup/2½oz/75g light brown sugar

4oz/100g flaked or ground almonds

Preheat the oven to 375F/190C/gas 5.

Start by preparing the crumble topping. Put all the ingredients into a large bowl, then rub together with your fingers until you have a rough, crumbly mixture that resembles coarse breadcrumbs.

Heat the dates, plums, lemon juice, spices, and date syrup in a saucepan for five minutes or so, until the fruits start to soften. Tip into a large heatproof dish and spoon over the crumble topping to cover the fruit completely.

Bake for 20–30 minutes until the topping is golden and the fruit is bubbling at the edges. Serve warm, with a dollop of ice cream or the Custarde Lumbarde (p. 105) custard.

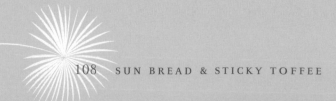

Fragrant green cardamom, grown in India, has a warm, musky aroma with lemon undertones. A little goes a long way with cardamom and the Romans used it to make perfume as well as cure bad breath. In addition to its essential role in rice dishes like biryanis, its soothing aroma is used to flavor chai and coffee throughout India and the Middle East, and a cardamom-infused sweet bread, *pulla*, is baked as far north as Finland. This desert is subtle and delicately date-flavored.

Cardamom Dream

DATE AND CARDAMOM-SPICED CRÈME BRÛLÉE

SERVES 4

4 cardamom pods

2 cups/16fl oz/450ml/ extra-heavy/double cream

⅔ cup/5fl oz/150ml whole/full-fat milk

5 large egg yolks

¼ cup/2oz/50g fine raw/golden caster sugar

2½oz/75g dates, chopped

raw sugar, e.g. demerara, for topping

Preheat the oven to 320F/160C/gas 3.

Crush the cardamom pods with a mortar and pestle. Pour the cream and half of the milk into a saucepan and add the crushed cardamom. Bring to boiling point, then remove from the heat, cover with a lid, and leave to infuse for 30 minutes.

Meanwhile, whizz the dates and remaining milk together in a food processor until well combined. Pour into the cream and cardamom mixture and when it has finished infusing, return the mixture to the heat. Bring back to a boil, stirring constantly to avoid the mixture catching.

Whisk the egg yolks and sugar together in a large bowl until pale. Strain the date cream into the egg yolk mixture, removing any cardamom pods and tough bits. Stir well.

Place four ramekins in a deep baking pan or high-sided roasting pan. Ladle the mixture into the ramekins, leaving ½ inch/1cm clear at the top. Carefully fill the pan with boiling water to come half-way up the ramekins, cover loosely with foil, and bake for 30–35 minutes or until just set. The center will be slightly wobbly.

Carefully lift the ramekins out of the pan, place them on a wire rack to cool, then move to the fridge to chill for at least two hours.

When ready to serve, sprinkle the sugar over each ramekin and caramelize with a domestic blowtorch or under a hot grill.

This recipe is inspired by a creamy porridge recorded in the Babylonian palace diary. When serving the porridge to important guests, they would have added dried dates to liven up the dish. Sun drying fruit, dating from the 4th century, was the earliest method of preserving foodstuff around the Mediterranean. This is a slightly more decadent topping, with the addition of almonds, star anise, and vanilla. It's delicious on porridge, served with a dollop of thick Greek yogurt, drizzled with a little honey, and whatever fresh fruit is in season.

Babylonian Breakfast

DATE, STAR ANISE, AND ALMOND COMPOTE

SERVES 4

7oz/200g dates, chopped

3oz/80g almonds, chopped

1 star anise

½ vanilla pod, seeds scraped

1 tbsp date syrup

Place all the ingredients in a saucepan, add 1¼ cup/300ml of water, and cook over low heat for 20–25 minutes until all the ingredients are well combined, soft, and sticky. Discard the star anise and vanilla pod and serve with yogurt and fruit or spooned on top of creamy oatmeal/porridge.

Palm trees grow in great number over the plain, most of them of the fruit-bearing kind, from which they make bread and wine and syrup. They are cultivated like the fig-tree in all respects. The natives tie the fruit of the male-palms, as they are called by the Greeks, to the branches of the date-bearing palm, to let the gall-fly enter the dates and ripen them, and to prevent the fruit from falling off.

Herodotus, **The Histories**, 5th century BC on date palms and fig trees in Babylon

Arid climates keep it simple. In the Gulf, a nomadic lifestyle and the scarcity of fresh produce meant that dates were mostly enjoyed simply, fresh off the tree. The Gulf's sweet dishes almost exclusively celebrate the fruit and another ingredient, readily available in times of war and peace—wheat flour. *Tamriya*, *afoosa*, *aseeda*, and *batheeth* are all date-based desserts popular in the region, delicious in their rusticity. The addition of flour provides bulk and nuttiness, with ground cardamom or a luxurious strand of saffron or two bestowing flavor. *Tamriya* is one of the simplest desserts to make but always a comforting classic.

DESERT DATE FUDGE

SERVES 4

1 cup/5oz/150g all-purpose/plain flour

9oz/250g dates, finely chopped

⅔ cup/5½fl oz/165ml vegetable oil

handful walnuts or almonds, roughly chopped, to finish

Tip the flour into a large saucepan and toast over low heat, stirring regularly, until a nutty aroma rises and the flour turns golden brown. This process takes around 15–20 minutes and cannot be rushed, or the flour will burn; it is essential to the end result.

Carefully pour the vegetable oil into the toasted flour and stir until you have a brown paste. Add the chopped dates, then mix well with a wooden spoon (a metal spoon will get hot very quickly) until incorporated and the bottom of the pan is clean. This will take a few minutes, as you mash the dates up into the flour paste.

Take off the heat and divide between four plates. Sprinkle with the walnuts and serve warm with cream or simply on its own. To reheat, return to the pan with a drop of oil.

The date palm has its feet in water and its head in the fires of heaven

Old Arab proverb

Al-Baghdadi wrote his hit medieval cookbook *Kitab al-tabikh* (Book of Dishes) in 1226, at the height of Abbasid sophistication and power. It included this recipe for *hais* or date sweetmeats. The dish has a long and illustrious history; it was thought even the prophet Muhammed enjoyed it. More importantly, this simple no-bake, one-bite dessert was said to "fortify the traveller" in the days when travel, especially the arduous journey to the Hajj, were often perilous. The original recipe says to "make into cabobs," which I took to mean small balls, but you could roll into finger-shaped sweetmeats or spread the mixture onto a baking sheet and cut into squares. Any which way, they are yummy and energizing.

Hais

DESERT ENERGY BALLS

MAKES 10–15 BALLS

5oz/150g dates, roughly chopped

2oz/50g almonds

2oz/50g pistachios

1 tbsp vegetable oil, plus extra to bind

handful toasted sesame seeds, dried shredded/desiccated coconut, or chopped pistachios

Whiz the dates, almonds, pistachios, and oil together in a food processor until ground and resembling breadcrumbs.

Tip into a large bowl and shape into balls roughly the size of a walnut (they don't need to be the same size). If still crumbly, dab your palm with a little vegetable oil to help bind the mixture. Place the balls in the fridge to set.

To finish, roll each ball in sesame seeds, coconut, or pistachio slivers, if desired—the options are endless.

Elche's Moorish palmeral is Europe's largest date plantation and,
since 2000, a UNESCO World Heritage Site. In the 12th century,
just before the Christian reconquest, there were over a million palm
trees here and the town was famous for its dates and pomegranates.
Today the shady palmeral is a haven of tranquility, ancient water
channels running through it and children playing nearby. The trees'
white palm fronds, grown away from the sun, are used to create
woven art.

Andalucia

Traveling south from Alicante to Seville, Andalucia's landscape is
strewn with evergreen palm trees. While I was melting in the June heat,
the trees seemed to be thriving. I took dozens of photographs of eye-
catching balconies with elegant palm fronds tied to them with bright
ribbons, remnants of Semana Santa, holy week, celebrations, when
even more fronds decorate the region's bridges and streets. Cordoba's
Mezquita cathedral, once a mosque, stands on rows of pillars in the
shape of towering palms.

23

In 1513, Spanish conquistadors carried palm seeds to Cuba hoping to start a palm plantation. However, the tropical rainfall didn't suit the tree and it never grew successfully. The small town el Datil, Cuba, is all that remains of that expedition. Their seedlings packed, the Spanish continued north to Mexico and California, leaving behind a trail of palms. The trees fared better in those drier regions, but growing dates from seedlings was a challenge until the 1850s, when offshoots were introduced for cultivation. Dates are still used in some Mexican desserts, like this one; ricotta fritters are also a popular Italian dessert. If you have a pastry/piping bag with a star-shaped tip, you can make these in the shape of the Spanish breakfast treat, *churros*, which are served with thick, sweet chocolate sauce or sprinkled with sugar.

The Conquistador's Treat

DATE AND RICOTTA FRITTERS

MAKES 10 SMALL PANCAKES OR 20 *CHURROS*

1¼ cups/6oz/175g all-purpose/plain flour

¼ tsp baking powder

2 tbsp superfine/caster sugar

1 tsp cinnamon

8 tbsp/4oz/100g butter

scant 1 cup/7fl oz/200ml skim milk

2 large eggs, lightly beaten

4oz/100g ricotta

4oz/100g dates, very finely chopped

vegetable oil, for frying

raw sugar, e.g. demerara, for sprinkling

Place the flour, baking powder, sugar, cinnamon, and a pinch of salt in a large bowl. Heat the butter and milk together in a large pan until the butter has melted and bubbles begin to form. Quickly remove from the heat and pour into the flour mixture, stirring until smooth and shiny. Leave to cool slightly.

Add the eggs, one at a time, followed by the ricotta, beating until smooth after each addition. Stir in the chopped dates, making sure they are evenly distributed throughout the batter, which will be thick and sticky.

To make pancakes, place a large frying pan over medium heat. Grease the pan very lightly with melted butter or vegetable oil, then ladle a few tablespoons of the batter into the pan for each fritter. Cook for 45 seconds on each side, until lightly golden. Keep warm until ready to serve, then sprinkle with the raw sugar.

To make *churros* (ridged, finger-shaped doughnuts), spoon the batter into a pastry/piping bag with a star-shaped tip. Fill a deep pan with oil and heat to around 375F/190C, or until a small piece of dough dropped into the oil rises immediately to the surface. Pipe the batter into the oil in 1½–2in/4–5cm strips and fry until golden and cooked through. Drain on paper towel and dust with sugar to serve.

Foodie friends suggested this classic Iranian sweet to me. This well-liked date slice is also popular in the Gulf, where the name is simplified to *rangeena*. Originally from Shiraz, it is prepared a little differently there: the dates and nuts are finely chopped, mixed, and then covered with the flour paste. Everywhere else, the stuffed dates are positioned upright. Cooking the flour and butter first allows the wheat's nuttiness through and once the ingredients are combined, takes this from rustic to chic. *Rangeenak* means "the colorful" in Farsi, probably in reference to the pistachio green and golden walnut filling.

Rangeenak

SHIRAZI DATE SLICE

SERVES 8–10

11oz/300g dates, pitted

2oz/45g walnuts, halved lengthways

2 tbsp sesame seeds

½ tsp ground cardamom

14 tablespoons/7oz/200g butter

scant 1½ cups/7oz/200g all-purpose/plain flour

chopped almonds or pistachios, to finish

Carefully slit the dates down the center, with as small an opening as possible to fit a piece of walnut inside. Squeeze it shut into shape.

Position the stuffed dates closely together in a square pan or ovenproof dish, either upright or side-by-side. Toast the sesame seeds in a pan for a minute until fragrant and golden, then scatter over the dates, along with a sprinkling of ground cardamom.

Melt the butter in a wide saucepan set over low heat. Add the flour and stir with a wooden spoon to combine. Keep stirring for about 15–20 minutes, until the mixture goes from a grainy texture to a liquid paste and from pale to light caramel. It may bubble, so keep stirring, as it can catch.

Carefully pour the mixture over the dates, using a spoon to ensure every date is covered and the mixture is spread out into the corners. Sprinkle with the chopped nuts and leave to cool for a few hours until set.

Slice and enjoy with a cup of deep red, unsweetened, tea.

Ice Cream,
milkshakes, and
stuffed dates

During the last football (soccer) world cup, my local *gelateria* got in the spirit by creating flavors for all of the countries competing. Brazil's Caipirinha, England's Pimm's, and Italy's Limoncello ice cream, and for Algeria's valiant efforts, a luscious date gelato. Ironically, while dates and scorching heat are plentiful in the Middle East, date ice cream is not. In granita- and gelato-loving Sicily, where the Arabs introduced iced desserts in the 9th century, ice cream artisans have been busy experimenting with flavors, textures, and recipes. In the town of Noto, about 56 miles/90km from Catania, *gelato di datteri* is on the menu, as are other exotic flavors like jasmine, bergamot, cinnamon, and one of my other favorites, pistachio. As gelato is generally made with milk rather than cream, this rich, creamy creation is technically an ice cream, and exceptionally good.

DATE ICE CREAM

SERVES 8–10

7oz/200g dates, chopped

2½ cups/20fl oz/600ml extra-heavy/double cream

14oz/397g can condensed caramel or dulce de leche

1 tsp vanilla extract

Place the dates in a saucepan with ¼ cup/60ml of boiling water and heat gently for a few minutes until the dates soften. Remove from the heat and leave cool slightly before blending in a food processor to a purée. Remove any tough bits.

Whip the cream to soft peaks, then stir in the condensed caramel and vanilla. Pour in the date purée, combining well.

Pour into a freezerproof container and freeze overnight or until solid. Take out of the freezer about 20 minutes before serving to soften slightly.

Dates are usually put into broths, mince-pies and restorative cullices, as tho they were of great and wholesome nourishment

Dr Moffet, **Health Improvements**, 1655

Every February near Palm Springs, California, the Riverside County Fair and Date Festival welcomes thousands of visitors. Since 1947 the 10-day event has celebrated the end of the date harvest in the Coachella valley, the largest date-producing region in North America. In keeping with the fruit's Arabian roots, the festival hosts camel and ostrich races and a spectacular Arabian Nights pageant, crowning a queen Sheherazade. Along Coachella's Highway 111, the date milkshake has become an iconic drink; some date farms serve up to 300 shakes a day. Delicious, and good for you, too.

DATE, SESAME, AND ESPRESSO MILKSHAKES

SERVES 2

¾ cup/14fl oz/400ml 2%/semi-skimmed milk or rice milk

7oz/200g dates, roughly chopped

4 scoops vanilla or date ice cream or frozen yogurt

Plus

1 tbsp sesame seeds

Or

1 tbsp instant coffee or espresso powder

Or

2 tbsp smooth peanut butter

Blend all the base ingredients and any additional flavorings together for a few minutes until smooth. Divide between two tall glasses and savor!

If dates and milk make the perfect food, the date shake is a gift from heaven

Jeffrey Steingarten, **Vogue**

Like prunes and apricots, dates are a big player in Moroccan cuisine, particularly in tagines and sweets. Popular date varieties include the helawi, deglet noor (originally from Algeria), and the king-of-dates, the medjool, once reserved for Morocco's royalty and guests. Sticky, dense medjool dates are considered a delicacy and are expensive due to their labor-intensive cultivation. In the 1920s, a deadly disease struck Moroccan date palms. Several healthy offshoots were sent to California to try and rescue the variety, where thankfully they thrived. Today the Moroccan town of Erfoud, a few hours south of Marrakesh, hosts a yearly date festival—three days of dancing, music, and food—to celebrate the date harvest. Stuffed date combinations are very pretty on a plate, or put on skewers and dipped in white or dark chocolate.

One-bite Date Feast

CHOCOLATEY STUFFED DATES

MAKES 25

25 dates (around 9oz/250g, or 22oz/625g if using medjool)

almonds, peanuts, pistachios, walnuts, pecans, mascarpone, blue cheese, lemon or orange rind, and/or preserved stem ginger, to stuff

9oz/250g dark or white chocolate, chopped, to coat

Ground pistachios, dried shredded/desiccated coconut, and/or sesame seeds, to coat

Slit the dates, lengthwise, and carefully remove the pits. Replace each pit with your chosen stuffing, then squeeze it shut into shape.

If you want to coat the dates in chocolate, melt the chocolate in a heatproof bowl set over a pan of barely simmering water. Place each date on a skewer, then dip halfway or fully in the melted chocolate to coat.

Leave to set on wax/greaseproof paper or roll in the pistachios, coconut, or sesame seeds. Best at room temperature.

Page 144: Dates filled with mascarpone, pecan, lemon rind, ginger rind, almond, orange rind, dark chocolate, milk chocolate.

Index

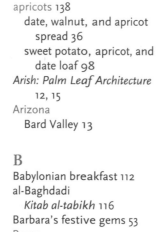

Acknowledgements

I am grateful to many friends and collaborators who helped grow this book from seedling to leafy beauty:

Rosie Reynolds who cooked with me and kept me sane, Jacqui Caulton for a gorgeous, sun-drenched design, Kate Whitaker and Cynthia Inions for creating beautiful food images. Once again, my good friend Monica Meehan was instrumental in getting me published and her calming presence throughout was invaluable, Jana Gough, always full of enthusiasm and positivity for my work, and my visionary publisher Michel Moushabeck at Interlink.

A big thank you also to the generous Alexandra Karan, Sarah Cobbold for editing the recipes, David Hearn for organizing the production, and Ori Hellerstein who baked with me.

Friends and family who graciously tested recipes at home and sent feedback: Barbara Erckman, Ghadah Al-Kandari, Petra Kwan, Muna Al-Mousa, mother-and-daughter teams Laila Al-Hamad and Yasmine Magnoli Bocchi; Rania Jada and Nadia Merkel; Sophie Kazan and Florence Makhlouf— thank you!

Around the world, from San Diego to Tehran, date-loving friends kept this project well-watered. Some sent travel snapshots, others stories and press cuttings, many gave ideas and more feedback; including the above-mentioned, I'd also like to thank: Alawiya Ahmed, Mitchell Albert, Georg and Antoine von Baich, Ashley Biles, Elaine and Raymond Bishop, Jovanka Bozhinova, Kiril Bozinov, Graham Day, Jolyon English, Rabaa Faraj, Waleed Gumaa, Betty Al-Hamad, Malu Halasa, Lazslo von Hoffman, Saniya Iskander, Rose Issa, Safa Mubgar, Vittorio Muolo, Suzanne Press, Rosalind Rathouse and Khalid Assyb at the Cookery School at Little Portland Street, Betty Riaz, Francesca Ricci, Ali Al-Saleh and family, Razan Al-Saleh, Wasan Al-Saleh, Sonia Shalam and Danielle Sharbit.

In Abu Dhabi, I am grateful to Henrietta and Andrew Jukes for helping me plan a trip to Liwa and the Al Foah date company in Al Ain for a fascinating tour and many goodies.

Warm thanks to my family in Kuwait, especially Laila Al-Hamad, a great supporter of culture and my brother Ahmed.

From Gulf roots to English shoots, this work could not have flourished without the tireless support and discerning palate of Matthew Corbin Bishop.